ALCHEMY OF IMAGINATION

THE POWER OF YOUR MIND TO TRANSFORM YOUR LIFE.

SAMI MOOG

ISBN: 978-0-578-58725-7

You aren't the center of the universe. The universe is the center of you

TABLE OF CONTENTS

PREFACE

Thoughts become things. This adage has been repeated in one form or another through the annals of history. Across virtually every civilization, great thinkers and philosophers have been conscious of the notion that our thoughts, while originating in the mind, eventually become tangible reality. Popularized in the modern era under the banner *Law of Attraction*, this concept is nothing new or novel, and has been professed by many of the greats from Socrates of Greece to Tesla of America. In the modern era, transformation of thought to tangible form has become a subject for discovery in academic, new age, and even religious circles. Although the idea sounds wonderful — that we can simply think of something and *voilà! There it is!* — this metaphysical principle has on face value proven to be substantively more complex and mysterious. Like most things in life, however, the answer is far simpler than it appears, echoing Confucius who is reported to have said: "life is so simple, yet we insist on complicating it." These words, spoken by one of humanity's most enduring cultural and philosophical icons, are absolutely true. Life is incredibly straightforward, yet we insist on complicating it.

Alchemy of Imagination explores the deep metaphysical principles of consciousness, and its relation to the external world. It seeks to guide you on how to effectively engage with your subconscious to draw out of the universe unparalleled prosperity. Life is difficult, and no one is born into this world with an operator's manual. This is why the vast majority of us see life as a battlefield. We fear that which we do not understand, and yet life is so much simpler than we currently conceive. While every soul's journey and mission are unique, there are universal principles under which we all operate. Alchemists of every stripe have been trying for a thousand years to turn lead into gold, yet no one has yet succeeded. Whereas that recipe may never be discovered, an equally important alchemical process exists in the chrysalis of thought to material reality, and with it you can turn the lead of your circumstances into gold.

No matter where you are in life, and no matter how dire your current circumstances, there is no valley too deep and no chasm too wide for salvation to reach you. Salvation is always close to us, yet oftentimes we go years without achieving it. No matter how cold the winter of your life may be, you must know that you have the power within you to change every trying circumstance in your world, and that power is available to you right here, right now. We often create for ourselves a prolonged period in our suffering because we misuse the awesome power of our subconscious, and we allow repeating patterns of failure to show up in our experience, over and over again. *Alchemy of Imagination* can awaken you from your imaginative slumber and enhance the alchemical power of your mind to transform your life into one of untold openness and abundance.

We live in a universe of law and order, and chaos has no rightful place in our life. Think about the mathematical precision of the workings of the universe. A realm that scientist now tell us is more than thirteen billion years old, this universe has evolved to such a heightened degree of mathematical precision that our scientists, with their technologically advanced computers, can now only scratch the surface of what makes our universe tick. You are not here by accident, and the events which occur in your life are not haphazard. God created you with incredible power, and although God is certainly a God of miracles, He is not in the business of spoiling us, but rather wants to lift us up and teach us about the powers He has given us. One of the reasons why repeating cycles of hardship keep occurring in your experience is because you are misusing your mind, and the moment you learn how to effectively wield your mind as the bio-technological miracle that it is, is the moment your entire experience in this world will begin to drastically improve. We live in a benevolent universe, created by a wonderful God. We were not simply created alongside the universe, and later placed in it — the universe and everything within it was created for us.

Quantum theory teaches us that everything is in a state of change, and everything resonates at a frequency of vibration. Our present state of being likewise resonates at a specific vibration, and through the proper use of our mind we can alter that state of vibration. Whatsoever we think in our conscious mind is impressed upon our subconscious, and that impression is then projected upon our field of view, or our sensory experience of this world. Although there is a time delay between our conscious imaginal act to its fruition in the field of view, the fact that our imagination manifests before us is true beyond doubt.

The ideas, concepts and techniques elaborated on in this book are influenced by some of the greatest thinkers in New Thought.

Napoleon Hill, Neville Goddard, Joseph Murphy, and others have influenced my understanding of the nature of reality, and the power of my own imagination and subconscious, like constellations in the night sky that guide travelers in every direction. The building blocks explored herein collectively harnessed and resolutely applied can be transformative in our daily lives and serve as a powerful methodology for achieving our aspirations, inner contentment, and spiritual appreciation of the world in which we live.

CHAPTER 1

IMAGINATION

"The power of imagination makes us infinite"
—John Muir

Since the moment you took your first breath, you have been thinking. None of us can remember anything prior to two or three years old, but we were alive nevertheless. Once we started to transmute visual and aural phenomena into syntactical meaning (i.e. language), we began to think coherently and precisely. Imagination is something we simply cannot turn off. Like breathing, thinking can be done consciously or unconsciously. If you so choose, you can breathe deeply, methodically, for any predetermined numbers of seconds in and out, but eventually your mind will become distracted and your breathing rate will return to normal. Even while you sleep and are totally in the realm of the subconscious, your lungs will continue to contract and expand because breath, like imagination, is directly tied to Spirit and cannot be turned off. The more you train your body to breathe slowly, deeply and consistently, the more it performs that function without conscious effort. Furthermore, the more you train your imagination to be uplifting, grateful and purposeful, the more frequently it will perform automatically without your conscious redirections.

While awake, thoughts are continuously being beamed from your mind; while you sleep, you are dreaming. Most of us, especially in the digital age, default to fast-paced, anxious thoughts. This has become our "normal." If you're anything like the rest of us, you can think happy and productive thoughts until life distracts you, and *bam!* you're back to the hustle and bustle inside your head. Like your breath, you can train your consciousness to be more empowering to you and over time, with consistent effort, it will become your natural, default state of being.

Because the external world is manifested directly from your imagination, this gift from Spirit is the most powerful tool at your disposal to effectuate a highly prosperous and enjoyable change or, alternatively to carry you to the depths of the earth buried under sorrow and hurt. Your imagination and its direct influence upon your life cannot be overstated, and the more you fully comprehend this truth the better equipped you will be to overcome every obstacle in your path.

Everything in your external world is a manifestation of your internal makeup. Your thoughts, feelings, assumptions, beliefs, and personality have all contributed to the makeup of your life down to the minutest of detail. Thoughts become things, and the mental images you hold in your neocortex eventually become a play-by-play in the visual cortex. Everything you once thought about, with belief and conviction, has manifest in the three-dimensional screen of space; everything that occurred in your mind as a passing thought, daydream or mental impulse has also manifest in your life as the backdrop to the overall circumstances of your experience. Once you grasp this concept and truly believe, as if it were real — and it *is* real — you can begin to wield this awesome power to your benefit. You can improve your health; get rid of painful, crippling issues from within your body, by focusing on healing using the step-by-step methodology. You can increase your wealth and receive abundance from sources you could have never imagined. You can relieve sore relations with loved ones, and so much more, if you only learn to wield the incredible power of the imagination properly and stop letting yourself drift into useless and unproductive daydreams.

What Exactly Is Imagination?

Imagination is the fabled breath of life, breathed into you by our great Source, Spirit, God. Imagination emanates from the deepest part of your subconscious and bubbles up continuously, from the depths of your soul, up through the filters of your heart, and finally into the conscious awareness situated in your active, aware mind. From there, you have the power to direct your thoughts to go in any direction you choose. Difficult at first, like weight-lifting, this becomes easier and more powerful through continued development.

Your imagination emanates from the unseen realm. Some say that our consciousness is like a radio antenna, tuning into imaginal wave patterns which already exist in the ether. Others claim that we ourselves produce these mental images. Either way, our imagination comes from something far greater than our three-dimensional, electrically charged brains. Imagination is non-material in nature, and this does not emanate from the material plane.

Think of imagination like raw power: like electricity, or steam. This power is, as said, raw — it is an expression of pure energy and without focus or direction it will prove useless at best, and harmful at worst. Think of electricity: Benjamin Franklin discovered electricity, but he did not invent it. That is to say electricity was always there, and Franklin simply discovered how to harness it for use by people. Lightning would still strike trees, homes and people, and was at best useless, and at worst harmful or deadly. That is similar to your imagination — an electrically conductive steam engine of greater energy than any of us can truly fathom — and your mind is the valley of power lines, which you can extend to any destination you so choose.

Through the effective use of your imagination, you can accomplish anything and everything you desire in life. Everything must be achieved first though the mechanism of imagination, and everything that necessitates the materialization of your desire will follow, in a chain of events that will occur in perfect order and sequence.

Your imagination is the greatest gift God has bestowed upon you. With it you can direct your life in any way you deem appropriate. Because the human being was given free will, we can choose to direct our reality in any direction we desire, and God has chosen to respect our free will so long as we tarry on the earth. God, through the mechanisms of the universe, will not hesitate to enact for us the constructs of our imagination, as this is universal law. What we imagine we become; what we imagine we receive; what we imagine we are. Imagination is undifferentiated energy that can be directed at will, and yours is the responsibility to utilize this unseen nuclear reactor effectively.

Imagination is the foundation of all experiences in our world. Nothing that has ever been discovered or invented was not first constructed in someone's mind. Benjamin Franklin did not discover electricity by accident; he had deliberately pondered on the nature of lightning and devised a mechanism by which to attract it to his famous kite. The Wright brothers did not create the airplane by accident; they had focused on their dreams of flight and devised numerous attempts to lift us up into the sky. Their minds constructed the reality of flight before their hands did. Thomas Edison constructed the idea of a bulb from which light emanates and long before light bulbs came into being. Likewise, you have probably already been thinking of taking control of your life and improving your conditions before opening this book. Your very own imagination led you to these pages, and you will be led far beyond, in due time and in good cheer.

That, dear readers, is your imagination. It is a power plant of endless supply, and when combined with focused desire and faith, it is able to construct your every imaginal act no matter how seemingly impossible it may seem. Your imagination will bring everything into its proper place without you needing to know the mechanisms. Whatsoever you imagine, with focus and belief, will come into being because within you is the universe and the universal supply of endless abundance.

What you imagine with consistency is projected onto your field of view, otherwise known as the screen of space. The reason this doesn't always seem apparent is because we so often think contradictory thoughts, and flow through endless states of being in a given day. What we experience in our field of view is a projection of the sum total contents of our subconscious, which is populated by the imaginal acts we hold in our conscious mind — the good, the bad and everything in the middle. Once you hone-in on your power, and imagine with precision, you will begin to see your entire reality shift and the projection of your subconscious will be exactly what you desire.

We all know what the human body is comprised of. We are a combination of certain minerals, organic matter and water, and theoretically it wouldn't be too difficult for scientists to synthetically fashion a compete human being. Yet, this corpse would be exactly that — a corpse, with no life, personality or capability of thought. It would be a dead body, albeit a synthetic one. The fact that we are alive, conscious, and have the capacity to imagine all that we can imagine is proof that the deeper part of us stems from another world and not simply this three-dimensional plane. Our imagination comes from Heaven, and with it we can lead ourselves to our own personal heaven on earth or hell on earth. The choice yours and yours alone.

Taking Responsibility
Perhaps one the most frustrating steps to taking control of your life is realizing that you yourself are the sole architect of all your misfortunes. Once you come to terms with this truth, and only then, will

you be able to manifest all your desires and more. You are not here by accident — nothing in this universe is. Your current circumstances are the culmination of all your positivity, negativity, love, anxiety, fear, jealousy, hope, despair, and confusion. Once you deeply ponder this statement, you will come to realize how much time you have wasted daydreaming, imagining conflicting desires, feeling anxious, and worrying about everything that could possibly go wrong. If it's any consolation, you're not the only one doing this. Most of us — in fact probably all of us — are living in this paradigm, because it's easy to slip into this mental attitude. This way of thinking is a downward slope, and downward motion takes no effort. The reason why so many of us are swimming in the ocean of our own created misfortune is because that is unfortunately our natural inclination. Just as gravity naturally pulls everything downward, so too is our imagination pulled downward into this three-dimensional plane, and with it all of the problems and confusions of the world.

You aren't a bad person, nor are you weak-minded. The game of life is a difficult one, and without constant reminders, we are all prone to this downward momentum of thought. However, your problems are your own fault, and no one else's. The universe isn't out to get you, and neither is God; neither are your co-workers, and neither is society. When you know that your life is always going to be the perfect culmination of your imaginal acts and feelings, you can finally be free from the powerlessness of your present reality.

This world is an ocean, and we are passing through. Each one of us is sailing on a ship of our imagination, over the sea of the universal mind. When our thoughts and imaginal acts are unfocused, dispersed, or in a constant state of contradiction, we will never reach any of our desired destinations, no matter how small or simple they may be. The ship of your soul will wobble in the vast sea of mind, being shifted to-and-fro by the undifferentiated currents beneath. You have the power to raise your sail, fortify your hull, and lift your anchor, but all of this takes persistence on the imaginal plane, as well as focus.

Our lives are the result of all that we have thought. Our relationships — romantic, platonic and professional — are subject to the way we believe others will treat us. Change your beliefs about how others will treat you, and others will treat you differently. Change your beliefs about what is possible for you to achieve, and you will move mountains. You don't need to know *how* your desires will come to pass. Leave that to the infinite mind that is the foundation of your imagination. You do not need to know the mechanism by which everything will fall into its proper place — the universe will arrange everything you need and all you must do is impress your subconscious by asserting your imaginal acts. Your subconscious will then project itself outward on to the screen of space — your field of view. That's it. Do that, and you will feel the pleasure of knowing that all your desires have been fulfilled because of your own conscious decision to utilize your imagination the way God has always intended you to.

Imagination Fulfills Itself

In order to more fully grasp this idea, let me bring to you an analogy. You are a soul, given free will and access to literally an infinite supply of abundance. However, for the time being you are placed in this three-dimensional construct and boy is it dark in there. Sure, we have the physical sun which allows us to see everything around us, but for the time being we are living without a spiritual sun. We can only see what is physically in front of us but not what is spiritually in front of us. Everything that is around us, but which we cannot see, is known as the unseen. The unseen is not the empty space in the universe, but the spiritual plane which contains everything and more, but is invisible to us for the time being. Although you are placed on this earth with seeming limitation you are actually given innumerable, metaphorical houses to live in, and you can choose to live in any house you so desire. Not only that, you can move to any residence you desire at any time and for any reason. What's more, when you decide to move, you are there. Instantly. Instantaneously. Completely.

It was mentioned earlier that within you is a nuclear power plant capable of igniting any amount of electricity. Without the requisite power lines, that electricity is dispersed and is not utilized, and so a bit of infrastructure needs to be built. Although you are able to move into any home you choose, and although everything contained within that home is yours for the taking, to enjoy or detest, all the lights are off and you have no perceivable access to any of it. Once you engage in the imaginal act of your choosing, you are there. There are no ifs, ands or buts about it. You are there spiritually, and it is all yours in the present moment. However, you can't perceive any of it and so it seems like you're still in your old house, with all of its comforts or difficulties. As you continue to engage with your imagination deliberately, accurately, and with passion your imagination will, without you needing to know how, begin to build and extend power lines from the power plant of your subconscious to the home of your field of view. The moment those power lines reach your new home is the moment your desired imaginal act is manifested into your perceivable reality — and it is yours to enjoy, or to detest.

This fact cannot be overstated: you do not need to know how your imaginal act will come into reality. There is an infinite mind at work and that mind will take care of every minute detail, no matter the obstacles are in your way. All you must do is properly use your imagination, over time, and your desired state is yours to become.

This is truly the greatest mystery of imagination. Once you begin to consciously manifest, you will be utterly stunned at how your thoughts become reality. Even if you were given a thousand years to plan out all that needs to happen in order for your imagination to become reality, you would fall short of the infinite mind which is constantly materializing our inner state, perfectly, without pause, and harmoniously with all other people. There are no shipwrecks in the sea of the universal mind, as the ocean of infinite intelligence knows exactly how to carry each ship to its imagined destination perfectly and directly.

Put another way, there are no tangled power lines in all the innumerable houses of the human creation. The universe constructs everyone's path perfectly, directly, and without hindering the paths of others.

Thoughts! Are! Things!

This universal principle cannot be overstated. Everything you have ever thought, felt, and believed to be true is being expressed in your outer world, absolutely. Everything that you are, from your conscious mind to the depths of your soul, is being expressed in your field of view like a movie, and you are the main character. Your field of view is everything you see, hear, feel, smell, and otherwise perceive around you. Though seemingly stagnant, your field of view is constantly being updated according to the expression of your subconscious. Whatsoever you impress upon your subconscious, knowingly or unknowingly, will inevitably be projected in your outer world, or field of view. Everything in your subconscious mind comprises your own personal field of view, and your field of view is always the exact and perfect representation of your subconscious.

The entire world is nothing but a mirror, reflecting back to you that which you truly are. Every encounter you have ever had with another; every uplifting word you've heard; every loss and every gain, is but a reflection of your thoughts, feelings and beliefs about yourself and the world. At every moment in time, you are shown a snapshot of who you are. Or, at least, who you *were*, as there is a delay in the manifestation of the contents of your subconscious.

Manifestation

Just as icebergs are water, crystallized, floating in water, so too are you a mind crystallized, floating in universal mind. In the same likeness, your material world all around you is your imagination crystallized, floating in a sea of your imagination, which will later be crystallized.

When using a buzzword like manifestation, it becomes important to define precisely what is meant. Manifesting is the flow chart that begins in the imagination and ends in your material field of view. Everything that occurs in your imagination winds up right in front of you, physically, whether you realize it or not. Said another way, everything in your awareness in this present moment is the result of all that you have imagined, visually and emotionally. This is key, because many people assume that only what is deliberately focused upon is manifested, and this couldn't be further from the truth. Everything that occurs in your imagination is manifested before you, in the exact likeness by which it was imagined. This goes back to the idea that you must take responsibility for your life, as everything you have impressed upon your subconscious, through the mechanism of imagination, is expressed.

In our early education we learned that energy can be neither created nor destroyed, only transformed from one form to another. This is very important to understand when getting ready to manifest something, whether tangible or intangible. You are not creating anything new with your thoughts, but rather crystalizing what already exists in a state of raw, potential energy. There are various names for this process. Some call it dimension-skipping — using your thoughts to travel across dimensions until you reach one where your desire exists; others call it the Law of Attraction, whereby your thoughts magnetize to that which already exists in the universe. Regardless of the name, it is the same phenomenon. You are using your thoughts to bring into your personal awareness that which you desire.

If you have ever thought about a person and hours or days later that specific person somehow appears in your life, then you know what it is to manifest. If you've ever woken up on the wrong side of the bed and seem to encounter every possible inconvenience for the rest of the day, then you are wholly familiar with manifestation. Manifesting is the bringing about into our awareness the sum energetic total of our thoughts, feelings and beliefs, and this power can never be turned off so long as we are alive.

Whether manifesting is an art or a science is up for debate, but my personal belief is that it is a bit of both. There is a precise mechanism by which you can draw into your life that which you desire as well as fear, and yet this objective reality which is ultimately grounded in physics must be subjectively experienced in order to be measured. No scientist, at least at present, can measure the vibrational difference of your environment due to the emanation of your thoughts. Yet, when you begin to develop a strict awareness of your conscious output you will experience a notable shift in your reality.

Synchronicities

Manifesting something into your life is both an art and a science. Though there is a precise mechanism you use to draw your desires onto the canvas of your awareness, only you can measure the results. Over time and with consistent practice, you will astonish yourself at how frequently you witness your imagination in physical form. You will also become more and more accurate as you sojourn on the path of attraction. For most people, the first few months are the most difficult, because they find themselves surrounded with the problems of the past and present and must hike upward toward the shining city on the hill of their imagination. This is key to understanding: there will *almost* never be the instantaneous crystallization of your desires into form. I say *almost*, because when an instant manifestation occurs it will usually appear in the form of a synchronicity rather than a completed manifestation. Synchronicity is a hallmark of the manifestation process. When a synchronicity happens once, we would call that a coincidence. When multiple coincidences occur, we call them synchronicities. When you deliberately manifest your field of view, the first thing you will notice are synchronicities all around you, and this is a sign that your field of view is beginning a radical shift. One type of synchronicity is that we have a passing thought and moments later it comes to pass, such as thinking of an old friend and then seeing an Instagram request from that very same person. Another type of synchronicity is when you decide to manifest money, and you visualize abundant wealth, and over the following days and weeks you find pennies, dimes and paper bills everywhere you go. You park at the meter with an hour of time left over from the previous car; you are offered a free cup of coffee by your barista. These are small indicators, or synchronicities, that your wealth is actively manifesting upon your field of view.

Manifestation is a Lifestyle, Not an Act

Thus far, you should have a grasp of the power of your imagination. If you can solidify that understanding as an unwavering belief in the deepest crevices of your being, then everything that follows in this book will be easy for you. You must accept that your imagination has the power to make or break you, and you have full and complete control over your imagination. Utilize it to its fullest potential!

At its most basic level, the precise mechanism of manifesting can be boiled down to a handful of steps. Certainly, if you want to create the life of your highest dreams, you will have to go above and beyond these initial baby steps, yet every great mansion is built upon cornerstones. Without the proper foundation, nothing built above it will last. I would encourage you to constantly refer back to this chapter, especially as you initially begin to change your life, because repetition is the name of the game when it comes to influencing your subconscious. Master these techniques to the point where they become second nature to you, and you will have mastered the foundational basics of energy work.

Manifestation is more than a technical act. It is a lifestyle, one which encompasses everything from attitude to belief to concentrated and dedicated mental action. The biggest breath of fresh air that comes with this law is that no effort needs to be undertaken. In fact, the more effort you force onto a situation, the more it will persist; likewise, the more effort you force onto a situation in order to make it happen, the more its fruition will be delayed. Imagination is the master key, and everything you impress upon your subconscious through the mechanism of imagination will appear in your life. It cannot be any other way.

It Takes Time

It is both a curse and a blessing that our thoughts do not manifest instantly. It is a blessing because, let's face it, your life would be a disaster on top of a train wreck if every thought you ever had was manifested the moment it was expressed. It is also a curse, however, because there is enough of a delay that we become unaware that we are the directors of our life. The delay in manifestation is sufficient to keep us unaware of our power, and therefore many of us are destined to a life of continually repeated mistakes due to wrong thinking. Everything takes form according to its predetermined schedule. The mustard seed will not blossom according to the timeline of the acorn. The gestation of the human being is nine months, distinct from the hatching of a bald eagle. Likewise, all of your imaginal acts gestate according to their predetermined timeline, and although you may not always be privy to those timelines, you can be sure that there is an appropriate season for all things in your life, and whatsoever you imagine will come to pass no sooner and no later than its appropriate time.

Three Steps

Although the process of manifestation is very nuanced and takes time to master, it can be boiled down to three, simple, foundational steps. Everything else builds on top of these steps. This checklist, while short and concise, is proven through the test of time, and is strong enough to build upon throughout the remainder of this book. Regardless of the situation, it is this three-step process that will effectuate the greatest change. In the following order, you must: *visualize*, *believe*, and *release*. Seems easy enough, right? Wrong. Thinking about visualizing is different than visualizing. Thinking about believing is even more difficult than actually believing. Letting go, or releasing is perhaps the most difficult, although it is very easy for us to simply think about letting go. When we're in the crosshairs of life, and a certain situation is causing us immense stress and grief, believing that your imagination will absolutely fix every problem you face, with haste, and then letting go of all anxiety is a monumental task, albeit a necessary one.

These guidelines will be accompanied with real-life stories in order to help you understand not just how to execute this methodology in your own life, but to emphasize the importance, accuracy, and efficacy that imagination has upon your life. Remember, in order: visualize, believe and release. Visualize, believe and release. Visualize, believe and release.

CHAPTER 2

VISUALIZATION

"Don't you know yet? It is your light that lights the worlds"

—Rumi

The three-step process is so integral to your use of the principle of manifestation, an entire chapter is devoted to each of the principles. The correct understanding of these principles is the difference between success and failure in everything that you do, become and receive in life. Master these techniques and you will begin to master your life — and you can only master these techniques once you develop right understanding.

Of the three steps, visualization is the easiest to master. You will thus welcome the fact that visualization is actually the most important step in the process. The word *visualization* is one you might already be familiar with and refers to the process of imagining what you desire, with consistency, until it appears in your life. Visualization is the exercise of your imagination. Using your mind's eye, preferably with your physical eyes closed, you must consciously and definitively develop a scene which implies that your desire has already been fulfilled. Perhaps one of the greatest mistakes people make in this endeavor is unknowingly visualizing the wrong scene in their imagination.

Your subconscious, though a powerful aspect of your being, acts more like a robot than anything else. Whatsoever you impress upon your subconscious via imagination will be expressed in your life at a future time. Given that fact, choosing exactly what to visualize seems daunting at best. Your subconscious takes every scene you create literally, and executes those images with perfect precision, every time, no matter how much destruction that reality may or may not bring into your life. It takes both contemplation and practice to get it right every time. To manifest correctly, you must visualize what I call the *afterthought*.

Creating the Afterthought

The most important piece of advice I could give you when talking about visualization, is to create the afterthought. The afterthought is an imaginal scene which details what would happen if your desired manifestations had already been fulfilled. In other words, if what you currently desire had already been fulfilled earlier today, yesterday or even last week, what would you be doing right now? That is the afterthought. Perhaps the best way to convey what I mean is to give you an example.

If you are trying to manifest a job, what type of scene would you construct in your imagination? Before you continue reading, take a moment to create a short, concise clip in your mind's eye that would imply to your subconscious that you want a job. For those of you who are already employed, do this anyway. What sort of scene have you created? The truth is, every single person reading this sentence has constructed a unique scene in their mind's eye, and this is why we all have varying results when it comes to manifestation. The only way you can manifest employment, if currently unemployed, is to *create the afterthought*.

When creating the scene in your imagination, you must imply that your desire has already been fulfilled. Again, this is the most important piece of advice I have to offer in this chapter. If you are looking for a job, and your visualization exercise consists of sending out job applications... take a guess as to what you will manifest. No matter how much you try to raise your vibration (to be discussed later); no matter how much positivity you infuse into your imaginal scene (also to be discussed later); because you chose to visualize sending out job applications, that is what you will continue to do in your waking life: more job applications. If you visualize yourself being interviewed, that is all you will manifest.

As already noted, your subconscious won't take even an iota of time to determine "what you meant." Your subconscious, though extraordinarily powerful, is robotic in its output. What you imagine is exactly what you receive. If, in this same scenario, you chose to imagine yourself shaking the hands of a hiring manager and being welcomed to the interview, that is exactly what you will manifest. Visualizing a happy introduction to an interview won't manifest your employment. You must create the afterthought. In order to land a job, you should visualize yourself signing the job offer. Certainly, you can think of your own afterthought — it doesn't need to be signing the paper. You can manifest yourself receiving your first paycheck with the company's name in the corner of your cheque. Any scene which implies that your desire has **already** been fulfilled is the correct scene to visualize. The imaginal scene must directly imply that your desire has been fulfilled, and thus you will manifest a situation in which your desire is fulfilled. If you visualize anything prior, that is where your manifestation will end — prior to the fulfillment of your desire.

The fact that you are signing the offer of employment; or the fact that you are receiving a cheque with your name on it, received from the company you desire to work for, implies that you are employed. Visualizing a scene wherein you meet with the hiring manager; or you walk down the halls of the company, does not imply that you are employed there. As has already been mentioned, those imaginal acts will definitely land you an interview and after that interview you will find yourself walking down the halls of the office just as you had previously imagined. However, walking down those halls as an employee rather than just a visitor is an entirely different story.

Creating the afterthought is absolutely key and cannot be understated. Let's bring another example to your awareness. Say you are recently single or dating someone and want to be married. What would you visualize? Now that you have a basic understanding of what it means to create the afterthought, think to yourself what an appropriate imaginal act would be before continuing reading. Take another moment to think about all the wrong visualizations you could construct.

It would be incorrect to visualize your partner proposing to you, because proposals can be broken off prematurely. It would be incorrect to visualize your wedding night, because many would-be brides or grooms will experience cold feet. It would be correct for you to visualize your own hand, with a wedding ring or wedding band on your ring finger. This is the *afterthought*. This scene implies that you have **already** received your desire. It is yours. It is received. It is finished. If you wanted to get back together with your ex-lover, and you put all your energy toward visualizing receiving a text message, that is a faulty approach because that it exactly all you will receive. From there, of course, you can continue to visualize each next step, but inevitably you will fail to reach your ultimate desire because our wisdom and understanding is so limited that we simply cannot comprehend every step that will need to happen in order to marry your former significant partner. By visualizing the outcome after the final scene, you are letting God fill in the blanks. Everything that must happen in order for your created afterthought to occur will occur in the simplest and most natural way. If there is any work to be done in the middle, you will be inspired to take those courses of action, and whatsoever others need to do in order for your wish to be fulfilled, they will do unbeknownst to them. God is the one orchestrating the affair, and God is the one who, through the universe and your own subconscious, will then manifest your visualization exactly as it was seen.

You must accustom yourself to always think in terms of fulfillment. What would you be thinking if and only if your desires were already fulfilled? How would you feel if you received your desire yesterday, or last week, or an hour ago? In real life, ask yourself what you would be doing were your desire already in your hands — and then create an imaginal scene in accordance to that state, and your desire will soon be yours, in the flesh. Though this takes some time at first, because your logical mind will need to actually think about what would imply the fulfillment of your desire, this should become second nature with enough practice.

Always see your desire as having just been fulfilled, in the immediate or recent past. Visualize what you would see, think, say, feel and do, in the afterthought of your wish fulfilled.

Imagining in First Person

Another crucial requirement of successful visualization is witnessing your imaginal act in first-person point of view. The reason for this is simple: because your subconscious will express outwardly what you visualize inwardly, it is imperative that you visualize from the proper perspective. If you've ever played a video game, you likely know what I mean by first-person point of view. Most video games have the option of viewing the gameplay from first- or third-person point of view. In third-person point of view, you see the back of your character, and as you move your character across the screen, you see him running, or moving his arms, as if you are slightly above him. You see the clothes he is wearing move according to the character's body movements, and you otherwise see the figure from a slight distance.

31

That is third-person point of view, and that is how most people visualize. Unfortunately, most people are doing it wrong, and are living with its unintended consequences.

When you wake up in the morning and you open your eyes, what you are seeing is life in first-person perspective. When you look down and you see your arms, hands, and feet, you are witnessing those body parts in first-person perspective. When you watch an old home-movie and you see your nine-year-old self dancing and jumping on the bed, you are seeing yourself in **third-person**. This is the difference. In first-person point of view, you see the world through your own eyes. You don't see yourself at a distance. You don't see yourself looking down at the wedding ring on your ring finger. You just look through your own eyes at your ring finger, and you see a wedding ring. A great and innumerable amount of manifestations have gone awry due to the mistake of visualizing everything in third-person point of view.

To continue with the example of marriage: if you close your eyes and look at yourself at some distance, and you see yourself looking down at your wedding ring and admiring the fact that your wish has already been fulfilled, what you are actually doing is creating an imaginal act of witnessing a person who is married. Because your subconscious expresses exactly what you imagine, perfectly and precisely every time, by visualizing in third-person point of view you have created a situation where you see another person married. This witnessing of another person married will occur in waking life, at some future point, and it is only because your subconscious expressed exactly what you impressed upon it via your imagination. After the advice of imagining the afterthought and nothing else, this is perhaps the second greatest piece of advice in visualization.

With eyes open, and with this book in one hand, look down at your other hand right now. What do you see? With your peripheral vision you see your forearm and possibly your biceps and shoulders. If you are laying on a couch, you probably see the fibers of the furniture a few centimeters below your hand. Do you notice the lines on the back of your hand? Do you notice any beauty marks? Do you notice your knuckles? All that you notice is being visualized in first-person perspective, because that is how we see life in our waking existence. That's why you do not see yourself in your room, laying on a couch. You don't see your legs outstretched, or yourself looking downward at your hand. You just see your hand, and with your peripheral vision, the surrounding area. Whenever you visualize, maintain that perspective, always.

To return to our example of seeking employment, let's envision signing the job offer. How would this be imagined, in the mind's eye? You would simply feel yourself seated on a chair, with the contract lying flat on a desk. You would feel the smoothness of the polished wood (or whatever material is relevant) under your arm, and you would look down and see your hand holding a pen, signing the paper. What you should not visualize, is seeing your entire body seated at the desk, signing a paper, as if you were witnessing a video recording taken of you at the moment you signed the employment offer.

Short & Concise Wins the Race

When visualizing, we should always keep our imaginal scenes short and concise. Oftentimes we will create grand scenes implying our wish fulfilled, spending upwards of ten minutes or more creating an entire movie in our mind's eye. Many people do this thinking a long, detailed scene will evoke the emotions necessary to propel their thoughts into the universe, but without any doubt, this is the wrong methodology. The shorter the scene is, and the simpler its construction, the more accurate its expression in the physical world will be. Going back to the marriage example — I illustrated the setting of looking down at your hand and seeing a wedding ring. That's it. Short, concise and simple. Whatsoever you imagine, will be played back to you in the real world, and everything that must occur in order for that imaginal scene to become real will occur in its proper sequence. The benefit of keeping your imaginal acts simple and short is that not only will you be able to replay them consistently in your mind over and over again, but they will be easier to impress upon your subconscious because it is easier to believe something simple, and belief is a core tenet of manifesting.

The more complex your imaginal acts, the more impossible it will be to repeat the scene in your imagination — and it is important to focus on exactly what you want and keep from that scene in your imagination until the seed of its fulfillment has been planted. When your imaginal scenes are too story-like, it becomes impossible to manifest your desires accurately, because each time you imagine the act, there will be contradictory details, details which were added or removed, and overall a messy, unrecognizable situation will show up at your door. Keep it simple, and you will maintain accuracy. It's that simple.

Decisions, Decisions

I know many people who have said that for years upon years they have witnessed synchronicities in their life — the spontaneous mani-festation of something they thought of — and yet nothing they truly desire manifests in their life. They visualize this, and visualize that, and only the small stuff seems to happen. The culprit here is a lack of focus. One of the most detrimental states of mind, on par with pessimism and ingratitude, is the state of confusion. The mental *back-and-forth* is like bringing in a bulldozer into the garden of your sub-conscious. Every time you dig over here in order to lay the founda-tion of a new desire or state of being, you toss the dug-up earth on top of your recently planted seeds. Soon after, the bulldozer that is your will begins digging someplace else, tossing the newly dug earth into the place you just finished excavating! The going and coming of your desires is exceptionally detrimental to your manifestations, and creates a state of long-suffering, to use an old English word. Long-suffering means, in modern English, patient endurance in the face of a difficult state or circumstance. When you constantly change your desires and try manifesting new desires too frequently, your subcon-scious doesn't know what you want and so it brings you to a season of waiting and will keep you there until you know exactly what it is that you want. Until you are able to home in on your desires with laser focus, you will remain in your current state, indefinitely.

One of the not-so-true maxims of our time is "the grass is greener on the other side." As soon as we attain something, we think that something else is better, and yet it often isn't. There isn't a thing in life without its pros and cons, although without doubt some things lean heavier toward one or the other. What would you say of a person who is looking to move, and can't decide on whether to move to the country, suburbs or the city? We can all relate to this dichotomy. If you live in the suburbs, or even further out in the country, you know just how peaceful, beautiful and relaxing summers can be. Endless meadows and towing canopies in every direction bring a deep sense of purity and calm to the heart. However, life can get boring in the less populated areas, and certainly come winter, loneliness often sets in. Those in the city, who often long for peace and quiet, and the cooler temperatures of the country, enjoy the fun and liveliness of the city, day in and day out. If this person who needs to make a residential move can't decide on country or city, an endless stream of delays and frustrations will set in until a decision is made. Visualizing a beautiful country home every day for a week, followed by the visualization of a clean city apartment will lead to the cancelling out of both desires, and in return the sender of these contradictory thought waves will see the return of a messy conglomeration of circumstance.

Likewise, it is foolish and pointless to spend time visualizing a brand-new Mercedes-Benz today, and a BMW tomorrow. You will either get neither, and be forced to wait, or you will get a lesser car that you never directly desired, because confusion was your state of being, encapsulated in your visualizations.

A similar notion is often said: there's no point in sitting down and generating feelings of gratitude for one hour a day, when the other twenty-three hours are spent grumbling. The hour spent in gratitude is cancelled out, and what you are left with is a continuation of your circumstances. Long-suffering will be the name of the game.

Imagine how ineffective an employee would be if he started a new task every ten minutes, instead of starting a task, finishing, and then moving on to the next. No business would thrive if all its employees behaved in that fashion, and likewise no field of view will be beautified by your desires if you, the imaginer, are constantly shifting your focus to-and-fro. Imagine if you decided to write a book, and twenty pages in you decided to write another book on another topic. Twenty pages into that book you then decide to write a third book on a third topic. You get the picture. You would be left with a room towering with pages full of words, but completely meaningless at best, and burdensome at worst.

Once you are absolutely sure of what you desire, then pick it, stick with it, and manifest it. Even if you change your mind later, stick with it nonetheless. The universe responds very well to consistency, and you will not be disappointed in your manifestations in the slightest. Even if you think you might have made the wrong decision, you are never going to cage yourself in. The Law of Attraction is never halted and is never meant to be used just once. As soon as you receive your desires in the three-dimensional space, you must immediately restart the process according to your new desires. The game of abundance is never meant to end, and human nature dictates that it should never end. We are, by our nature, needy and desirous. Our desire will never be satiated and everything that we manifest will eventually become old and tired, just like everything else in this world. We live in a realm of indescribable abundance, and you should never fear that you are manifesting something that will actually make you feel bad. Everything you manifest is designed to propel you to your next stage in life; toward your next state of being. If you decide on manifesting a beautiful city apartment, stick with it. It will manifest in the exact likeness of your imagination. There are absolutely no doubts about that. Stick with it, and it will appear in your field of view. Once critical mass has been achieved, then begin manifesting your country home, if you so desire. That, too, will manifest, but if you waver between the two, unsure of which you desire more, unsure of which is better for you, you will only manifest a situation that brings about more confusion and insecurity. You receive what you put out: if confusion and contradictory imagery is your output, then more confusion and contradictory imagery is what you will receive.

Planting the Seed

The biggest question we all want answered is: how long will it take? The truth is, there is no definitive answer, yet in most cases, as soon as possible is the best possible answer. Some imaginal acts will take mere minutes to manifest, while others can take years. Most, however, will fall in the near-term range, and will occur at some point in the near future relative to when you are determined to create those realities.

It is common knowledge that trees of differing species will grow at differing rates. It is also common knowledge that if an acorn is planted, an oak tree will manifest. These two statements are as profound as they are simple and are integral to the understanding of manifesting.

Your subconscious can be likened to a plot of land. The soil of your subconscious is of infinite fertility, and no matter what you choose to plant, it will grow. Throughout our lives, we inevitably transform this barren plot of land into a lush garden, with trees and plants of every kind. What many of us fail to realize is that just as any physical garden needs constant maintenance, so too does the garden of our subconscious.

The question often arises: how often am I supposed to imagine a certain scene in order to manifest it in reality? Again, there is no exact number, and each manifestation will require a varying degree of frequency. A general rule is, the grander your request, the more often you will need to imagine it. That is precisely why we so often see something we just thought of an hour ago, or the day before — because the manifestation is small, and inconsequential.

The other day, I stopped by the gas station to fill up my car. The station closest to my house is a small, family owned gas station, and they usually offer the cheapest prices. I've lived in the same house for about twenty years, and since I first got my driver's license I've been filling up at this particular station. For some reason, while I was filling up gas this time around, I looked up at the large sign that showed the company's name "Excel." I remembered that years ago this gas station was owned by Texaco, an oil company which no longer has any stations in my city, but once had multiple. I actually remembered exactly what the logo looked like, with a large "T" overlaid on a large red star. This memory consumed my thoughts for a few seconds, and then I went about my day as normal. The following morning while I was drinking coffee, a link popped up on my browser showcasing photos of Northern Virginia, where I live, but back in the 1950s. As someone who loves anything historical, I immediately opened the link, and — I'm sure you already guessed it — a black and white photo of this very same Texaco gas station appeared on my computer screen (and, thus, my field of view). This isn't a coincidence, but rather a practical example of a small, inconsequential and nearly instant manifestation, as we're talking just a few hours between thought and synchronicity.

One of the core tenets of manifesting is that your manifestations will *almost* always flow into your reality through the smoothest and most natural mechanisms possible. Although miracles absolutely do happen; although God absolutely does "zap" our lives with some huge and unexpected windfall, this isn't the norm and it certainly isn't what we should aim for. God is not in the business of spoiling us, but rather in helping us lift ourselves up time and time again. If you were to watch a time-lapse of an oak tree grow from a mere buried acorn into a towering display of strength, you would be amazed at how it all happens according to a predetermined schedule. There are no quantum leaps in the growth of that oak tree — it doesn't jump from acorn to seedling to sapling to baby tree to mature tree. The oak tree consistently, steadily and seamlessly transitions from one phase to another, and the general rule is that your manifestations will appear in your field of view in much the same way: with rhyme and reason, and according to its season.

It's been mentioned earlier that everything you think about will manifest in your field of view, in the exact likeness of your imaginal act. This is a universal truth and is never turned off. It has also been mentioned that the norm is for your manifestations to be made visible at a point in the future, and not in the immediate present. Your mind is a garden, and your experience in this world is a direct reflection of your subconscious. All that you are is a result of all that you have thought, and your entire world is you, pushed outward.

Vividness of the Senses

When visualizing your afterthought, visual imagery is typically the first sense people employ. You want marriage, and so you *see*, in your mind's eye, your wedding ring. This is the case because visual imagery is not only the easiest sense to bring into a visualization, but oftentimes the most effective in terms of results. We do have, however, four other senses to choose from, and all of them should be infused in your mental imagery in order to supercharge your manifestation.

When visualizing your afterthought, or the moment *after* your desire has already been fulfilled, try to think about how that scene would feel. Earlier the example of signing an offer letter was used. Are you wearing a short sleeve shirt? If so, what is the texture of the textile, on which your arm is resting. Do you feel the metal clip on the pen touching your index finger? Is there light streaming through the window and warming your skin? How does your imaginal act *feel*? It is important to make your imagination as real as possible. Remember, this imaginal act will serve to create a real-life expression in the future, and so being as clear and concise as you can, using all the vividness of your five senses, will ensure maximum effectiveness.

Think about that same scene in terms of your other senses. Create a mental conversation in your imagination. Look directly at someone and have a conversation with them. What would you say to this person if your desire had just manifested in the immediate past? "Isn't it wonderful that…" is a good starting point. Remember, keep your imaginal act short and concise, not exceeding one minute.

If you want to manifest a trip to the ocean, try to remember what a salty ocean breeze smells like. How does it feel to be splashed in the face by the cool ocean mist? To have the sun over your head? Bring all of these senses into your awareness and construct your imaginal scene as if it were literally happening right now. The point of bringing in all of your senses is because when your imaginal act is so vivid that you forget that your eyes are shut and you aren't actually there, in your imaginal scene, your manifestation is sure to come, of that there is absolutely no doubt.

Visualization Works, Every Time

Visualization works every time. Of that there is no doubt. Over time you will recognize countless imaginal acts appearing before you in your field of view, so long as you commit yourself to impressing upon your subconscious all that you desire to have, do, and become.

When you have definitely decided what you desire and have constructed your imaginal scene with all the vividness of reality, in a short and concise scene, then you are sure to receive what you have expressed in your imagination, because it is universal law.

CHAPTER 3

BELIEF

"Believe you can, and you're halfway there"
—*Theodore Roosevelt*

Once you have imagined your desire, or your state of being which you aspire to achieve, you are done. There is no other possibility. Everything you play out in your mind's eye will be portrayed in your field of view, in the flesh, at a certain point in the future. No amount of repetition will be enough to drive this point home. By the end of this book, you should have an unwavering, unshakeable faith in your ability to manifest whatsoever your heart desires, through the medium of your imagination. History is replete with inventors who failed endlessly before they succeeded. We all know the famous biography of Thomas Edison, inventor of the lightbulb. Edison once said: "I haven't failed, I've only found 10,000 ways that don't work." This is the belief you must cultivate in order to enjoy the fruition of your imaginal acts.

Lack of belief, or faith in your own ability to manifest everything you imagine is the leading cause of failure to materialize your desires.

When you don't believe with utter certainty that you are receiving your imaginal act in the flesh, you are essentially emitting thoughts and feelings of lack, which directly contradict your imaginal acts of abundance and prosperity. It is the equivalent of contradicting your imaginal acts the moment you partake in thoughts of abundance.

What's the point of imagining prosperity for an hour each day, only to fill the other twenty-three hours with deep-rooted beliefs of lack and powerlessness? In all honesty, which do you think will overpower the other?

Ain't Nobody Got Time for That

The reason belief is such a powerful tool, either for or against us, is because it is a state of being as opposed to a specific imaginal thought. We live on planet earth, and responsibility comes with the territory. Given the fact that we need to sleep for approximately one-third of the twenty-four-hour period, that gives us a very limited scope of time to manifest. In all honesty, we don't have the time to spend hours on end each day imagining all the things we so desire, and that's where belief comes in.

Belief is a state of mind, a state of being. Belief in the generosity of God and the watchful eye of His Countenance; in the working of the universe in our favor and the abundance of the planet all around us; these are rooted in our core and when we integrate this understanding of reality into our subconscious, we will be in a state of perpetual manifestation. This doesn't mean that negative events will never happen — we live in a fallen world and there will always be challenges to surmount, but being rooted in the Divine mind, through faith and belief, will ensure that prosperity will always surround us, and we will have full access to it. Belief in our imaginal acts coming to pass in the physical supercharges our manifestations and creates an environment whereby we can receive our creations without any hinderances. Belief simply removes all energetic obstacles that are otherwise in your way. Without strong belief at your disposal, you will remain under the currents of life, being swung to-and-fro, with only your small manifestations coming to pass (because you believe small things are easy and therefore possible).

Assumptions

Within us are innumerable assumptions about life, and these have been developed throughout the course of our lifetime on this Earth. Many of these assumptions are to our benefit while many are definitely not. It is imperative that you root out any negative assumption about life which is based more on your subjective experience rather than in reality. For example, many people assume that they don't deserve freedom. These people think that they must have an arduous job to pay the bills, and when they are at home, they need to be responsible and take care of their loved ones. These people believe that personal freedom can and should only come in small bites, such as on a Saturday afternoon. This is an assumption and connected to it are all the reasons why we maintain that assumption. "It's the responsible thing to do…" or "it's just the way things are…" That assumption about freedom is based on the subjective experience of life, rather than on reality, and the proof of this is that there are many people in the world who absolutely don't answer to anyone and who live their life according to their rhyme and reason. Just because *most* people seem to maintain the *work-home-chores-bills* routine, doesn't mean that that's the way life needs to be. If you were to assume that total and unconditional freedom was your birthright, you will achieve it.

If a person assumes that he or she is unlovable, seldom will anyone love that person. Because you are a human being, created by God the most loving, by nature and definition you are the most lovable being in the universe. The former assumption is rooted, unfortunately in too many people, because of a series of subjective experiences, but the reality of the matter is quite the opposite. Those people we all know, who seem to succeed in their career, popularity and romance have a core assumption about themselves centered around love and self-respect. They believe they are worthy of love and respect, and thus assume that the world will shape itself around that fact. And it does, every time.

Assumptions can be the trickiest things to maneuver around, because they are often hard to discover. Assumptions are rarely something we consciously think about. We have no problem seeing the assumptions of others, but in ourselves is another task all together. Recognizing and clearing out all unnecessary and detrimental assumptions in our lives is a continual practice, and a necessary one.

Assumptions and beliefs are rooted together, and thus have the same effect in our reality. A core assumption about life will bring about a recurring manifestation — a repeating pattern, for better or for worse. Although we seldom think about our assumptions, they are responsible for most of our day-to-day reality, and that is precisely why our lives seems to remain the same on a daily basis. Our assumptions, and thus beliefs, are running the show, and our conscious imaginal acts are colorizing it. If you believe that you are totally unworthy of love, and yet you imagine going out on a date, you can bet your bottom dollar that your date — which will definitely manifest — won't go any differently than any previous romantic encounter. If, however, you imagine that big beautiful rock on your wedding finger, and steadily and persistently address your negative assumptions about the reality of love and companionship, your lifelong partner will be sure to arrive posthaste.

Seeing is Believing

It's easy to say to ourselves "I believe that I am worthy of X, Y and Z." It is another matter altogether to actually replace our lack of faith with unshakable belief in the unseen. Human beings are faithful by nature. Children will believe just about anything they are told and will hold on to it with all their might. The fact that so many of us, in our adulthood, are shrouded in pessimism and assumptions of lack and scarcity is a testament to the difficulty of this world. How exactly do we undress our souls from the clothing of negativity and fear? Like everything else in life, it's far simpler than it seems. Just as fear and the scarcity mindset crept in over time, so too can you force these beliefs out, over time. However, because you are now ready to proactively clean out the garden of your subconscious, this process won't take years or decades, but weeks or months.

Everything in this book up until this point has been explained in order for you to understand the true nature of our lives. It has been said over and over again that anything you imagine will come to pass in your field of view, at a certain point in the future. This is true whether you know it, believe it, understand it or not. Because we don't all have the time or wherewithal to consciously manifest every single desire of ours, perfectly every time, we must rely on the deeper mechanisms of our subconscious, namely belief. As mentioned, belief is centered around faith and assumptions — they are three in one, one and the same.

A straightforward way to develop your faith in universal generosity is to make a consistent practice of visualization. When you maintain your mind's eye on the afterthought, and when you keep your mental scenes short, concise and simple, you will begin to accept them as reality more quickly than you realize. Keep holding onto your dreams in the form of imaginal playwrights and your subconscious will readily play them before you in your field of view.

Another good practice is to simply recall all the times synchronicities occurred in your life. No matter how small, try to recall as many incidences as you can, where something or someone you thought of suddenly appears in your life shortly thereafter. If the Law of Attraction works for the small stuff, there is no reason why it shouldn't work equally as effectively on the big stuff. The more you practice manifestation as outlined in this book, the more you will see the reality of your imagination at work, thus increasing your faith each and every time you manifest.

Don't try and force yourself to believe — that will only make you neurotic and frazzled. Just know, in the depths of your heart, that you live in a benevolent universe, and regardless of what happened — or didn't happen — in your past, let it go and trust that taking full reign of your imagination is the necessary and transformative step to accomplishing every desire of your being. Faith will come so long as you remind yourself of all the times something miraculous occurred in your life, no matter how insignificant. You were guided to this book, and you will continue to be guided so long as you trust, believe and keep faith.

A Course in Faith

Do you believe that you are reading this book? Or, are you simply reading this book? In other words, you don't believe something when you can see it plainly before you. None of us *believes* that the sky is blue, we simply know that the sky is blue because it is right there for all to see.

When a toddler looks up at the bright blue sky, does he believe that the sky is blue, or does he know it. For sure, toddlers have an immense imagination, and having only spent a few years on this Earth, they don't really know anything for certain. It is only after looking up at the sky day in and day out, year upon year, that children *come to know* that the sky is blue.

Likewise, we *know* that the forests are green in the summer, autumnal in the fall, barren in the winter and lime in the spring. We have seen this pattern enough times to know that seasonal shifts are both real and predictable. The problem lies in what we can't see, and any physicist worth his weight in feathers will attest that what we don't see vastly outstrips what we do see. We've all been in chemistry class, studying the electromagnetic spectrum. That tiny strip of rainbow, dubbed "visible light" is what we see. We are visually blind to everything else on the spectrum. Thus, it's pretty hard for us to *know* things, isn't it? We can't really see anything save for a small sliver of the universe, and yet here we are, making judgements about the universe and our roles in it.

Many great sages have repeated the truth that we simply don't know enough to worry. In fact, legend says that on Lao Tzu's death bed, he was asked to give the sum total of his lifelong teachings, and he replied, "don't worry." We are in wonderful hands, of that I can assure you.

Because we are aurally and visually blind to nearly all of the electromagnetic spectrum, we must rely on our other, softer faculties, such as intuition and logic. Just as we know that forests go through seasonal changes multiple times per year, so too do our lives go through predictable changes. Ask yourself how many times you've woken up on the wrong side of the bed, only to find yourself delayed and frustrated at every turn for the next few hours. Everything seems to go downhill when you allow negativity to get the better of you (and believe me, we are all guilty of this). This is a clearly predictable pattern of operation.

Look back at all the times your imagination led to a creation or manifestation, and you will begin to notice a pattern that far exceeds the possibility of mere coincidence. It is precisely this pattern that should build your faith. If it happened once before, then it can happen again; and if it happened countless times before, then it will continue, forever in perpetuity.

Reacting is Futile

One of the chief poisons that keeps us in our state of lack is our constant reacting nature. Everything sparks a reaction in us, and this is a big problem. If you've been trying to manifest a new car and it's taking a long time, think to yourself what you think every time you drive your current car. If aggression, impatience or downright negativity occurs in your head every time you look at your car, no matter how terrible it may be, what you are doing is delaying the manifestation of your new car, which is yours by right because you have imagined it.

If you so desperately want to move out of your current home, and you've been imagining your dream home for so long, but every time you pull up to your home you think about how much you despise your current roommates, or whatever the problem there may be, you are delaying the new home which is certainly coming to you. Every time you negatively react to a situation, be it bad weather or the time it's taking to achieve your dreams, you are causing yourself a big delay.

The key is **not** to simply pretend like everything is perfect. Sure, you don't like your current car... that's perfectly okay. The problem lies in **reacting** impulsively every time you think about how long you've had to drive it, all the while wishing for a better ride.

The very fact that you react negatively every time you are reminded of your current situation is proof that you don't **really** believe your desires are being manifested. If you truly believed your dream home was just a short while away, nothing would bother you in the present moment. If you truly believed your two-seater convertible was on its way, regardless of the fact that you can't afford it today, you wouldn't be upset that you're driving your current car. You wouldn't have any doubt or fear that your desire simply won't show. You would be firm in the knowing that you are about to receive your desires in full, and in short notice.

As soon as you feel like going down that negative mental path, as you (and all of us) have so many times before, stop yourself prematurely, and remind yourself that you have the power to call into your experience all that you desire through focused and principled imaginal acts. You don't need to know how, when and through what mechanism your desire will materialize, because that is not for you to figure out. Your job is to simply wish for something, concentrate your imagination upon it with laser focus, and believe with utter certainty that it is coming, because you live in a benevolent universe and you are in good hands.

Game Plan

Going forward, believe. Even if you don't believe, believe anyway. Time will pass regardless, and so no matter how difficult it may be to believe that everything you imagine will come to pass exactly as you have imagined it, at a certain point in the future, believe anyway. Trust that your subconscious will respond to your new and improved thought patterns, and everything you imagine will come to you, as it always has in the past. Deep down, you know that your total experience at present is the sum total of all your past imaginal acts and feelings, and so make the determination to improve upon your imaginal acts, increase the frequency of positive imaginal acts, and believe with all your spiritual might that what you have imagined is already yours, and it will appear very soon.

Ask yourself this question: if I were in line to buy a lottery ticket, and angels from heaven descended and told me that the ticket I am about to buy is the winning ticket, would I feel upset or impatient that the person in front of me is taking too long to count change? If you knew, with absolute certainty and unwavering, infallible knowledge that the winning lottery ticket was yours to claim as soon as you approach the register, you wouldn't feel anxious in the slightest. You would simply be in a joyful state, knowing that immeasurable good is about to reach you. That, dear reader, is the belief you must cultivate in order to effect positive results from your manifesting practices.

You must develop the immovable belief that all the good you have imagined is being delivered to you, and you must only persist in your imaginal acts and belief and know and trust that you are in good hands.

The next time you find yourself in a situation where you are waiting for something you desire, but there seems to be life's typical inconveniences in front of you, just believe that it is all okay, and you are receiving what you desire. So just relax and keep faith.

CHAPTER 4

RELEASE

"They can do all because they think they can"
—Virgil

Up until now you have become accustomed to the first two principles of drawing from the universe all that you desire. Everything and anything that you imagine, with focus and mental attention, will be shown unto you again, in the flesh, in your field of view in the future. This is a universal law that is never altered. You now also know that your beliefs and assumptions about yourself and the world around you are the underlying energy your subconscious puts out, and your imagination essentially colorizes those subconscious constructs and plays them out for you in the form of repeating patterns in your life. There is a third and most crucial step in the manifesting process that is perhaps the most difficult to develop.

In Hindu legend, there is a story of a young girl who was walking through the marketplace with her parents. Suddenly she sees a bunny rabbit directly in front of her and manages to catch it. Immediately the young girl falls in love with the furry creature, and the thought occurs to her that she should keep this bunny as her pet, so she can shower the animal with affection and love. As she walks toward her parents, the young girl's mind becomes filled with doubt and fear that her parents won't let her keep the rabbit as a pet, and she will be forced to release it back into the wild. These fears cause an unconscious behavior whereby she holds onto the bunny so tightly that she unwittingly strangles the poor creature. By the time she approaches her parents, the rabbit has died.

Somber and miserable as that story is, it proves a very relevant point. The more we hold onto to our desires; the more we obsessively think about them and wish they were here, the less likely we are to receive them. Our obsessive desire essentially strangles our wishes before they are ever able to be fulfilled. Letting go and trusting God to grant you anything and everything you wish from Him is one of the most essential steps in manifesting your desires.

The idea of letting your desires go is a confusing one, for sure. On one hand, it seems contradictory to the idea of repeatedly imagining your wish fulfilled, and on the other it seems near impossible, because the mere fact that I desire something means that I haven't let it go. Once you gain a deeper understanding of what exactly is meant by letting your desire go, these issues and any other will be cleared up. For now, know that letting go does not contradict the principle of imagining your wishes fulfilled, and is certainly a possible feat for even the most obsessive among us.

Your subconscious will let you work just as hard as you believe you have to in order to attain your desires. Let go and apply the techniques outlined in this book, sit back and be amazed at your results.

Letting Go of Attachment

To be unattached is not to be numb or comatose with respect to your desires. It is to be content with the possibility of not receiving your desires. That is a very difficult concept to swallow, because the mere fact that we desire something implies that we are not satisfied being without it. Desire is a form of hunger, and our hungers of all kinds need to be satiated. Nevertheless, we are human beings, with souls, minds and free will. We not only have the ability but the responsibility to rise above our carnal nature and subdue our lower selves. Maturing is never an easy process, although it is an inevitable one. We mature, or life will see to it that we mature. When we desire something so terribly that we shake with anxiety and frustration when its coming is delayed, we are only constricting its arrival to the point of its miscarriage. We must convince ourselves that life will be just dandy without X, Y or Z. Only then, will our desires rush toward us headlong.

All of the world's major religions tell us to not fret over this world, and to relax and let it come to us. The more we try and desperately grasp the things of this world, the more they run away from us. It's like a Chinese finger trap. I'm sure you played with those as a child. A Chinese finger trap is essentially a hollowed-out fabric cylinder, and the game is to place both index fingers in either side. When you pull your hands away, the device constricts and locks your fingers in place, and yet when you relax and slowly push your hands together, the gap widens, and your fingers are released. That's a fair analogy for manifesting our desires. We must relax and go with the flow, recognizing that without our desire, we will remain perfectly okay.

This brings us to the idea of living in the present moment. When we are constantly worried about the future or ruminating over the past, we are not living in the present; and yet, while living in the present, everything is always okay. Except in extremely rare circumstances, the present moment is a very safe place to be, and we must always remember and recognize that fact, and not fret over the manifestation of our imaginal acts.

Don't Meddle in the Middle

Perhaps the most astonishing aspect of our ability to manifest is not in the ability itself, but in the way our manifestations come about. In the overwhelming majority of cases, our desires will become a reality in our field of view through means by which we could have never conceived. In nearly every case, our reality is constructed in such a way that goes against, or away from our plans or ideas on how life will unfold. As you start to witness your manifestations become reality, you will be amazed and astonished at the means that are employed for your imagination to become fruitful. Time after time, you will revel at the infinite intelligence at work, and you will be humbled. Over time, you will learn to happily let go of the means, or the middle, and simply rejoice that your desires will become your reality in some way that you cannot presently imagine.

Letting go of the *way* something happens is crucial to living a stress-free existence. Although you can certainly make plans, and certainly you can hope that a desire will come about in a specific way — and this will not hinder your manifestation in the slightest — you will nevertheless be overwhelmed by a Force greater than yourself. This Force — call it God, the universe, or Source — will always employ the simplest and most direct path from A to B; from your imaginal act to reality.

The fact that there *is* a middle is also an important point to note. As mentioned earlier, and as you likely already know, your imagination will not produce a spontaneous reaction in the sense that your desire will spontaneously materialize out of thin air. We live in a natural world, and there is a natural order to things. Although our imagination will materialize in the exact likeness by which we have imagined every single time, we should always assume that a natural chain of incidences will occur in order to bring that imaginal act into our present reality. The exact chain of incidences, however, is not in our hands — and thankfully so! Life would be infinitely more complicated than it already seems to be if we were responsible for planning and organizing every event and every chain reaction necessary to produce our desires in material form. Thankfully, we only need to create, in our imagination, the afterthought, and everything that needs to take place in the middle will occur in perfect order, no matter our plans or ideas of the matter.

Perhaps the most common example is the instance of winning the lottery. Everyone dreams of being one of the lucky recipients of that enormous, instant fortune. It's not the paper ticket that we want, but rather the giant cheque that follows. In other words, we want a fortune, and we want it now. Many people, upon discovering the immense power of their imagination, desire to manifest the lottery, and while certainly possible, the lottery ticket is not the afterthought, and thus most people never end up winning the lottery. When you decide that financial abundance is going to be the focal point of your imaginal act, you mustn't focus on the *how*. Winning the lottery is a middle event — a bridge between you in the present moment and your financial fortune that is manifesting in your field of view. You, a human being, have no way of conceiving the chain of incidences between you and your fortune, and so it is better to let go of the middle — winning the lottery, in this case — and simply imagine, believe, and receive your fortune in the way that your subconscious devises.

Continuing with that example, you might be thinking that winning the lottery seems to be the simplest and most direct way to achieve a fortune. And, on the surface it seems so, but there is a Force of incomprehensible wisdom behind your sail; and remember that God's kindness and generosity will never contradict His wisdom. If it is better for you to win the lottery, then the lottery is yours and no one else's. If, however, amassing your financial fortune is more beneficial when conducted through more conventional means, then your financial prosperity will enter your life through those means. Because you are given the gift of free will, you can choose financial fortune for yourself, and you won't be hindered whatsoever. You cannot, however, determine and force upon the universe the *how*. You cannot meddle in the middle.

From Believing to Receiving

Your ability to let go is proportional to how much you believe that your imaginal acts are truly your soon-to-be state of being. While distinct steps, each with their own purpose and outcome, the two are closely aligned. Believing relates more as to how strongly your imaginal act will appear in your field of view, while letting go relates to how smoothly, simply and quickly your imagination will become your reality.

Visualization is the first step in manifesting, and most assuredly the most important. Visualization is the act of your natural free will to determine what you will receive from the unseen. To use your imagination is a choice you are allowed to make, and there is no judgement from your subconscious with regards to the morality or lack of morality around your choice imaginal acts. While visualization is the first step in creating your future according to your free will, it is definitely a stand-alone act in the three-part process of manifestation. That is, visualization can bring you riches, but it can also bring you poverty. It is effortless, non-judgmental and non-biased. Believing and letting go, however, are more intimately connected to your spiritual progress and more biased toward your greater good. Whereas imagination can help or hurt you, the depth of your faith and your ability to let go of the outcome are directly correlated to the pleasantness of your future field of view.

Visualization determines what your field of view will develop into, as well as colorizes your deeply rooted beliefs and assumptions; belief determines how powerful your improvement in circumstance will be, as well as how accurate your imaginal acts will transmute into reality; letting go of the outcome determines how efficiently the universe will orchestrate your new reality into being, as well as shorten the time frame in most cases. Because you have surrendered and let go of the outcome, due to your deep and unshakable faith that it **is** coming, exactly as you have imagined, you are removing every stranglehold, every obstacle, and every blockage between you and your manifested state of being, desire or circumstance.

Don't Sweat the Small Stuff

Early practitioners of manifestation often relate that they always seem to manifest small, insignificant happenings but their true desires, the big ones, never seem to hold ground. This is a reality that shouldn't be denied, because it is true for all of us — at least the first part of that quandary. Why is it that the small things are so easy to manifest, and come so successively one after the other?

Take a look at the universe. We live in a truly blessed age, where we have visual access to the universe unlike every generation prior. In a universe that contains the Great Sloan Wall, supernovas so gargantuan that the mind cannot begin to fathom, and innumerable celestial objects many times larger and heavier than our own Sun, how can it be that anything we could wish for would be too large to produce? Sure, from our perspective, there is an enormous range between manifesting a cup of coffee as compared to a dream home by the water. Compared with what is contained in the universe, is that difference in any way comparable to what the universe has already produced, and in numbers beyond our ability to count? Moreover, in studying the modern global supply chain beginning at the coffee plantation and ending at your local coffee shop, you will realize that even manifesting a simple cup of coffee is in fact a huge feat for the human being. Nothing is small, and paradoxically nothing is big, either. The reason we reckon certain things small and others large is because of two reasons: our ignorance and our physical human limitations.

Because we don't consciously think about the grandeur of the universe day by day, we forget how astonishing it truly is. Moreover, we often fail to realize that what our astronomers have witnessed and shown us is far less than what the universe actually contains. We, in our human condition, become accustomed to the humdrum of daily life on Earth, and we inevitably place items, circumstances and wishes in categories of size and difficulty. We think, almost universally, that a phone call from an old colleague is easier to create than a seaside residence, and yet it isn't. The only determining factor in what is possible is what we imagine and believe to be possible.

We also fail to recognize the power of our imagination and belief because we connect our mind to our body. We think that because our bodies are limited — and certainly, they are — our mind and spirit too must be limited in similar likeness. This, fortunately, cannot be further from the truth. As long as our desire is possible through the limitation of this three-dimensional universe, it is possible for us to achieve no matter how seemingly impossible it may be. No matter the obstacles before you — and let's not deny that there absolutely are obstacles around all of us — you will be able to bulldoze right through them, through the power of your imagination and belief, and your ability to let go of the means by which your desire manifests in your field of view.

When you think of someone from your distant past and later that week that same person connects with you on social media, that event was manifested. We, collectively, have very few limited beliefs surrounding communications, due to the profound strides we've made technologically. That is why it is so easy for us to think about people, or images, from our past, and hear from that exact person or see that image on the internet.

Once you convince yourself that everything you imagine is possible and accept that the means by which that desire will materialize is beyond your ability to control or predetermine, you will see that small and large manifestations begin to flow into your life at near equal pace.

Timing

The fact that small and large desires are equally able to be manifested through the workings of your subconscious should now be a belief as solid as stone. Nevertheless, you probably think "well, sure, all is possible, but a house will take longer to manifest than a cup of coffee, right?" Usually, but not necessarily, yes. The fact that one manifestation may take a year, and another may take an hour is no indicator of whether it is possible and is still being created in your field of view.

Oftentimes we get discouraged when we plant the imaginal act in our subconscious, believe with unwavering certainty that it is possible, let go of the outcome, but don't see any sign of its coming for some time. The fact that we become discouraged is actually a sign that we haven't properly let go. It is no sign of hinderance that a specific manifestation is taking its sweet time to show up in your field of view. We must never forget that we live in a three-dimensional universe, and all things operate in and under time.

To truly let go means to let go of not only the mechanism by which a manifestation forms, but its timeline as well. We must also not go into our imaginal acts believing that because this desire seems so big, or seems to be surrounded by so many hinderances, that surely this one is going to be a slow one. Melting the belief of slowness with the imaginal act will be sure to produce a slow manifestation, because our reality is molded by our imaginal scenes and feelings, in the exact likeness of how the imagination was inwardly expressed.

The more you focus on time, whether during the initial imaginal act or during the waiting period that sometimes accompanies manifestation, you are resisting the process of letting go, and are bringing about more obstacles and delay, even if unwittingly.

Timing is something you can almost never predict, unless timing is built into the natural order of things. For example, if you are applying to a master's program in graduate school, then you know the deadline for submitting your application, you know the deadline from the school to release its letters of acceptance, and you know the date of orientation and the first day of school. In situations like that, then of course you know the timing and can predict when your manifestation will become the reality of your field of view. More broadly, though, you cannot predict timing because the middle is out of your hands. You cannot orchestrate the chain of incidences that need to take place in our orderly world for your desire to manifest, and so you cannot predetermine the timeline. You can, however, let go of your imaginal act and desire by asserting within yourself immovable belief in your ability to consciously design your life. Because you know, without certainty, that your imagination is the preview of life's coming attractions, you will not be bothered with trying to control how your manifestation comes about, and how long it will or won't take.

How Do I Know If I've Truly Let It Go?

We're all human and although we always *want* to do the right thing, we oftentimes don't know if we've actually done it or not. Sometimes it's hard to tell if you've actually let it go or not, but there is a definite way to determine whether your desire has been released into the competent hands of the universe.

In the previous section, the process of belief was explained, as was its importance and the consequences of belief. You know that with true belief comes the extinguishing of anxiety, fear and impatience. With letting go, another peaceful state comes about, and this state will be your gauge as to whether a true letting go has taken place.

When you have imagined your desire, or your state of being, and you believe with profound certainty that your imagination creates your reality with total perfection, you must now release it into the hands of the greater Force. When you find yourself focusing on your desire for a brief period of time — a day, week or month — and then you find yourself forgetting about it and immersed in a joyful busyness of your daily life, you can be sure that you have properly let go. This doesn't mean that if you think about your desire in any amount, you haven't truly let go. Rather, this means that when you find yourself joyfully preoccupied with your life and are not heavily focused on "where is it and when is it coming; why isn't it here yet" then you have properly let it go.

Whereas belief comes with the putting out of the fires of fear and stress, letting go comes with the casual forgetting of just how much you want or need your desire. It is less the forgetting of your desire, and more the forgetting of how badly you want or need it. To desire is strongly and completely as important when you are in the imaginal stage of manifesting, because that strong desire is the electrical current that flows from your conscious imagination to your subconscious. Yet, when that intense desire remains, or even grows, over weeks, months and years, then you have not properly or fully let it go and must do so in order for the stranglehold upon your manifestation to be released. Remember, it is not so much the forgetting of the actual desire that is necessary, but rather the peaceful, calm forgetting of the intensity of desire and need.

Another way to put it is that you become more patient with your situation of lack, and you stop reacting negatively to every reminder of lack. This enhancement of your patience is a sure sign that you have let it go, because you are no longer tying your manifestation down with your emotional intensity and negativity.

Reaction

When an inconvenience, no matter how significant or otherwise, shows up in your field of view, the most detrimental action you can produce is that of reacting. Instant, negative reactions to daily occurrences are responsible, more than anything else, to the reoccurrence of future inconveniences. More than that, immediately and negatively reacting to a situation is the surest way to ensure that the resolution to that event is slow and painstaking. A great example is traffic.

How many times have you been driving down the road and out of nowhere, just around the bend, you find yourself slowing down to a standstill, behind a long line of red brake lights? I guarantee you, with absolute and unshakeable assurance, that if you do not react to that situation negatively, but instead show sincere gratitude that the traffic jam isn't that bad, it will clear up, taking minutes at the latest. The reason I am so sure of this, is because I have made this a consistent practice in my life. And, it hasn't just worked most of the time, or nearly every time but every single time — without exception. The only caveat that needs to be mentioned here is that the feelings you present to the universe must be sincere and genuine. If you say in your head or out loud: "it's perfectly okay, this isn't a big deal" all the while you are clenching your steering wheel as if you're ready to rip it off, then I assure you the traffic jam will persist. If you genuinely don't mind the brief delay, brief it will be.

I use the example of a traffic jam because I have seen incredible success with that example. Because we're dealing with universal law, this principle must then apply to every other type of situation, whether a sudden inconvenience or a year's long struggle. The next time you are driving on a one-lane road and a heavy 18-wheeler cuts you off, don't let any negative reaction take hold of you and release all care about the situation, and watch as it makes the next available turn, removing itself from your way.

When you consciously override your natural inclination to resist, react and become frustrated, your salvation will not be delayed, and the problem will not intensify. You won't lose twice, when your free will to relax and let go can ensure that you win twice, hurrying the saving grace we all desire, while lessening the struggle in the meantime.

Let go of reaction in all circumstances: big and small; sudden and long-term. This may be difficult at first, but the moment you realize you have reacted, reverse course, and know that it is never too late to reverse course. Over time, your urge to react will diminish, and won't be second-nature any longer. The more you practice the art of letting go, the more it becomes your natural and consistent state of being.

Letting Go Relieves You of the Effort

There is a more practical way to gauge your level of detachment, and that is how much conscious, forced effort you are engaged in. You know that sometimes work will need to be done, but that work will be easy for you, and will be inspired. For example, you've been concentrating on a cup of coffee for free. Effort would be going to the dozen coffee shops in your town, one after the other, trying to force someone to offer you a free drink. Work, however, would be driving to your usual coffee shop at your usual time, and knowing that pretty soon, someone is going to offer you a free drink.

When you decide that you are ready to let your manifestation go, and be formed by Hands greater than yours, you may still have work to do, but no effort will be necessary. If you find yourself trying to conceive of ways to make it happen; if you are constantly going out of your way, thinking that you might be able to do something which catalyzes your desire into realty, then you are failing to let it go. Release it, work if necessary but produce no effort. If you have imagined it, aligning it with your deeply help beliefs of the generosity and abundance all around you, and entrust it to God to work through the universe and produce for you results beyond your imagination, then you have let it go.

Everything you imagine will come to pass exactly as you have imagined it. Whatever feelings and beliefs infuse your imaginal acts will determine how your field of view comes about, and letting it go will bring your manifestation right into the palms of your hands, with no effort or organized planning needed on your part. You must surrender to the joy of knowing that you are at the precipice of fulfillment, and the only gap between your present state, and your manifested desire, is the bridge of incidences which you must allow to naturally unfold.

No outside forces, people or circumstances are relevant to your manifestation coming to pass except the imaginal impressions you place upon your subconscious. Feel the feeling of the wish already being fulfilled, while meditating upon the afterthought; believe with compete assurance that you have the power to alter your present field of view with the power of your imagination, and let go of all attachments to the intensity of your desire, how it "should" come about, and how long it "should" take.

CHAPTER 5

MILE HIGH MANIFESTING

"All that you see in front of you is how you feel inside your head"
—Alan Watts

At this point, you have been shown everything you need to know about manifesting your desires. You have been made familiar with the concept of imagination, and its infinite power to create your reality as you wish. You have also been shown the power of belief and how assumptions run your day to day affairs. Letting go — perhaps the most difficult step in the three-step process — was also explained to you. Now that you've been given a thorough understanding of the manifesting process, I'd like to share a personal story.

I live on the East Coast, and I recently decided to take a spontaneous trip to Los Angeles. I've been there before, and I love it. The weather is outstanding and scenery second to none, with its cascading green hills and endless summer. Because this was a spontaneous trip, I didn't have much time to check with anyone regarding my travel plans. I was scheduled to stay in Los Angeles for about a week, in an AirBnb.

A few days into this incredibly fun vacation, I was told that my father, who doesn't live in the same city as me, was in town. I see my dad a lot and so if I didn't get to see him this time around, it wouldn't be the end of the world. Nevertheless, I wanted to spend some quality time with him. By now it was early Thursday morning, and I was scheduled to leave Los Angeles Friday afternoon, and arrive on the East Coast by late evening. I decided that I've already had plenty of fun, and it would be best to cut my travels short and return home immediately. I went on my airline's website to see available flights for Thursday, and to my dismay there were zero flights until Friday evening, hours after my originally scheduled flight. As someone who knows that imagination creates reality, and there are no obstacles before me that cannot be overcome, even under such time constraints, I decided to use the manifesting techniques outlined in this book. Keep in mind, I've used these techniques countless times before. I know it works and so this was nothing new to me.

I went into the bedroom, knelt in prayer and asked God to open for me a way home today. I know that when I connect to the Higher Power, all things are possible, and I am answered before I even ask. I then laid down on my bed for about a minute or two, and simply imagined myself back at home, feeling grateful that I was able to catch a flight home under such short notice. I imagined myself saying to my family the following words: "isn't it amazing that I was able to get a seat so quickly! I'm so happy to be home early."

Because I've brought myself to the imaginal plane so many times before, it goes without saying that there can be no distractions. I ensured that the balcony door was closed, the computer and phone were set aside, and I made a space for myself where I could be totally alone in my thoughts. I completely immersed myself in the imaginal scene, to a degree that I forgot I wasn't actually at home. After a couple minutes, I decided to call my airline's customer service number. I figured that I would have more luck speaking to an actual person rather than navigating the website on my own. The lady I spoke to on the phone assured me that there were absolutely no available flights, and there was nothing she could do to assist me any further. To be completely honest, I was a bit surprised, because I *knew* without any doubt that I was going home today. Not tomorrow as per my original plan, but today. There was no other way, because I imagined the scene with complete vividness and belief. The woman I spoke with then said that there was one available flight at midnight, which would have me arrive home at about 7:30am the following morning. This would be about 13 hours before my original flight, which would bring me home at 9pm that night. I told her that I wasn't interested in that flight, because I didn't want to sleep overnight in an airplane seat. I hung up and decided that someway, somehow, I would be going home, and I just don't know how yet.

Keep in mind, at this point it was about 8:30am in Los Angeles, and so there is a bit of a time crunch. My scheduled flight is the next day at 1pm, and I wanted to leave right away, and get home before night time on the East Coast. Given the time it takes to get through airports these days, that gave me a very short window to manifest my flight home. Nevertheless, I knew it would happen.

I had already planned a hike that day, so I figured I would hop in the shower and continue with my day as originally planned. I figured, best case scenario I leave today, worst case I leave tomorrow. If I don't end up manifesting a flight home today, it's no big deal and life will go on. I reminded myself not to care too much, and just let it go.

After I got showered and dressed, I decided to pack my suitcase and backpack. I wanted to show the universe that I was ready and willing to go home today, and I am going to prove it by packing all of my things and clearing out the AirBnb I was staying in. I cleaned up and set everything in order, as if I was checking out then and there.

As I got in my rental car and started driving to the mountain I was going to hike, it occurred to me that the midnight red-eye **was** my manifested flight home, and I should have at least asked how much the change fee would be if I took that flight. While maneuvering through Los Angeles' deadly traffic jams, I decide to call my airline's customer service once again. This time, I spoke to a different person, who told me exactly what the previous customer representative had declared: there are no available flights except the red-eye, which I was now told costs around $600, including the change fee and fare difference.

By now, I'm more than an hour outside Los Angeles and still on the phone. I explained to the customer service rep that I absolutely want to go home today, and there's no other way this call is going to end. He apologized and explained again that there was nothing he can do.

Suddenly — and I kid you not — he said, "actually, I'm now seeing that there is a flight leaving Los Angeles at 1pm today. A seat just opened up, but it will cost you $404." Now I was really surprised, because as confident as I am with my manifestations, it still tickles me every time it works. However, I know that when something is manifested, it falls into your lap, and there is no work to be done. I explained to the representative that $404 is simply too much money for me, and he then asked me why I needed to travel so suddenly. I explained to him the situation, that my father was visiting, and although I will see him for a few days regardless, I'd like an extra day with my family, and so I'd like to go home today and not tomorrow. The representative put me on hold while he spoke with his supervisor and returned and said that he would waive the $200 change fee, but I will still have to pay $204 due to the change in fare price. I said… "done! Book it!" The reason I so quickly agreed to pay the $204 is because my credit card company waives $200 spent on this particular airline, once per year. It's a promotional offer, but it doesn't go toward purchasing the original ticket price. It is only valid for in-flight purchases and ticket change fees. I only had to pay $4 out of pocket and that is good enough for me.

I literally manifested a plane ticket home within two hours of committing myself to the imaginal act, believing it is already mine, and letting it go. However, now I was faced with another problem.

It's now about 9:45am and I am more than an hour's drive from my AirBnb. In order to make it on a flight out of LAX at 1pm, I would have to seriously hustle. I would have to return to my AirBnb, gather my belongings, drive to the car rental lot to return the vehicle, take a shuttle bus to LAX and then get through security. A tall order for a short supply of time. Because I had already packed my belongings, cleaned the AirBnb and prepared for check-out, this proved to be my saving grace. I raced back, with full knowledge that I was going to make it on that flight because God wouldn't give me this opportunity only to watch me miss it, as long as I dedicate myself to fulfilling the manifestation as best as I can, working in the way I need to but without forcing effort into the situation.

By the time I got to the boarding gate it was 12:13pm, and boarding began at 12:20pm. I made it just in time, and I felt incredible. And that's not even the end of the story.

While I was on the phone with the representative, I asked him if it was possible to be given an aisle seat. I get very claustrophobic in most situations, most frequently on airplanes, and sitting by the aisle is a huge relief for me. Unfortunately, I was told that the one available seat, which I was purchasing, was a middle seat. However, I knew that I was sitting on an aisle seat. I imagined sitting by the aisle and also giving thanks for that new seat. I had included this in my original imaginal act earlier in the morning, and now I imagined once again sitting in the aisle on my flight home that day.

I was in the final group to board the plane, and so when I was walking down the aisle, I could see how fully booked the plane really was. When I approached my seat number, the lady sitting in the aisle seat next to me asked if I would mind switching seats with her husband, so they could be seated together. Without even asking which seat number her husband was sitting in, I replied in the affirmative, because I was already sitting in a middle seat toward the back of the plane, and so pretty much any other seat would be an upgrade. I'm sure you guessed it by now. Her husband was seated in an aisle seat, and that became my seat for the flight.

Manifestation, ladies and gentlemen. It works!

CHAPTER 6

HYPNOTIC IMAGINATION

"If you can dream it you can do it"

—Walt Disney

By now you have a solid grasp of this game called life, and how to play it. Everything you imagine will come to pass, exactly as you have imagined it. Once you picture the scene in your mind's eye, employing as much vividness as you can, developing a scene which would imply that your desire has already been fulfilled, you should believe it is already yours and then let it go. It's that simple. Given the fact that a day is 24 hours, one-third of which is spent sleeping, we only have so much time to imagine our afterthoughts. And, even under the best of conditions, we will still be negating at least some portion of our imaginal acts due to our hidden and latent assumptions, no matter how much we succeed in rooting them out. The question arises: how am I supposed to manifest everything I desire when most of my day is either spent sleeping, or engaged with the daily activities of the world? Fortunately, like everything else, the answer is much easier and more practical than you would think.

At any moment of the day or night, you can realize your wish fulfilled by imagining the afterthought, and these imaginal scenes will come to pass. There are, however, certain times when your subconscious is more susceptible to influence from the conscious imagination. For many of us, this has more often than not been a detriment, for we unknowingly use these times to negatively influence our subconscious, thus producing in our future fields of view stress and toil.

As you prepare yourself for sleep, laying down and closing your eyes, you are entering a short window of time when you are between worlds. The length of time varies from person to person, but typically there is a 15 to 20 minute window of opportunity, as your conscious mind dozes off into slumber, but conscious awareness is still there. During this time, before sleep overtakes, you have the power to influence your subconscious to degrees unreachable during other parts of the day, when the conscious mind is fully operational.

Your imaginal acts are given another boost of energy immediately upon waking, before full consciousness is restored. These two periods of time differ in what they allow you to achieve yet are complementary to one another. Whereas your imaginal acts in the moments before slumber take the throne are leagues more powerful than your oft-produced daydreams, your early morning imaginal acts are more short-term, and influence the day, rather than overall field of view.

When your mind begins to shut down, in preparation for its nightly sojourn into sleep, the barriers between the analytical mind and the subconscious are torn down. Bit by bit, the gaps between brain and mind, mind and soul, are dissolved, and every impression upon your subconscious is expressed multifold. This temporary, yet daily state can be likened to hypnosis. Though not as methodical, and with a different purpose, this nighttime dissolution of the conscious allows your imagination to penetrate the deepest realm of the soul, and what we focus on during these passing minutes has a profoundly powerful effect on our future field of view.

Think about all the nights you fell asleep to the tune of all your problems. Think about how many nights came and went to the songs of stress, fear and anger. Think about how many nights began and ended in sadness. Think about it and resolve never to think about it again. Resolve yourself to never fall asleep thinking about the stresses of life, but only of what you wish to impress upon your subconscious, with the aim of changing your field of view for the better.

It is my experience, and that of many others, that whatsoever you impress upon your subconscious during these final minutes of your waking consciousness will be more fully impressed as compared to imaginal acts done during regular hours of the day. It is imperative to take full advantage of this time, every day, because you will see your entire field of view shift positively in ways you can only currently imagine.

When you enter this semi-hypnotic state, your imaginal scenes are able to bypass the two gatekeepers of the soul, namely, your analytical mind, and your beliefs and assumptions. Part of the reason that so many of us have trouble accurately manifesting that which we desire to see in our field of view is because no matter how vividly we imagine a specific scene, our imagination is discolored by self-defeating beliefs and assumptions of the world, as well as the overriding logical mind that reminds us of all the reasons why our desires could never happen. Whatsoever you imagine will come to pass, absolutely and perfectly. Because our visualizations are so often produced to the tune of disbelief and dismay, we manifest exactly what we imagine — that is, not receiving what we were imagining. We insist on manifesting a home by the water, all the while coupling that beautiful visualization with thoughts of impossibility. The acorn of our imaginal act is planted in a field of thorns.

When entering this state between wakefulness and slumber, as we do each night, our imagination may slip past these otherwise watchful gatekeepers. Because the conscious mind is in the process of shutting down, the normal bombardment of all the reasons why we can never achieve our desires is quieted. Our visualizations are able to take root in the valley of unconditional acceptance, and belief in its coming will sprout forth very quickly.

It is said that whatsoever you contemplate before sleep will repeat like a broken record throughout your sleep. In the 1990s there was a children's cartoon called *Dexter's Laboratory*, starring a boy genius with a secret laboratory in his room. Everyone else in the cartoon is more or less ditzy. In one episode, Dexter desires to learn French, and he wants to learn it in a hurry. Instead of taking classes at school, he decides to fall asleep wearing headphones, with a tape player repeating commonly used French sayings. As soon as Dexter is about to fall asleep, the CD skips, and becomes stuck on a three-second loop, repeating the worlds "omelette du fromage," or cheese omelette. Unbeknownst to Dexter, this single phrase repeats until morning, and Dexter wakes up having forgotten how to say anything and everything except "omelette du fromage." Dexter now has to re-learn English all together. Though funny and obviously hyperbolic to the extreme, this scene actually proves an excellent point, relevant to the idea of manifestation. What you visualize to yourself, in the form of self-talk, visual scenes and feelings, before falling asleep, will continue on repetition until awakening. Though not as direct and instant as the example played out on *Dexter's Laboratory*, over time the effect is essentially the same.

Hypnotic Visualization

Though a three-cylinder, 1967 vehicle with a leaky engine will get you around town as you run your errands, wouldn't you rather drive a brand new eight-cylinder turbo convertible with a shiny coat of paint? Of course, that would be preferable. The fact that you are able to get around town is necessary but getting around town in style is an option.

Likewise, conducting your imaginal acts throughout the day will, without any hesitation, produce your manifestation upon your field of view, yet only with inner toil and self-improvement. You know that beliefs and your rational mind are the gatekeepers to your subconscious, and a certain degree of perfection must be achieved in order for your visualizations to appear in your experience as you desire them to. Not to cause any misunderstanding — everything you imagine will come to pass, but because we are human, with limited capacity for self-awareness, oftentimes our imaginal acts are unwittingly studded with assumptions, beliefs and feelings of being unable to truly achieve. We imagine our desires exactly as we wish to experience them, yet the accuracy of our manifestations is sometimes subpar, because our visualizations are tainted with disbelief and dismay.

Getting out of that old, broken down car and into your new V8 convertible is a conscious choice — one which entails properly utilizing the moments before sleep to your advantage. Manifesting during the regular waking hours is both advisable and necessary. Manifesting in the semi-hypnotic state before sleep is multifold more advisable and necessary, as this will not only turbo-charge the speed by which your manifestations materialize, but more importantly the degree of accuracy to which your coming field of view matches your imagination.

One of the most time-consuming steps in manifesting your desires is changing your beliefs and assumptions. Whereas you can choose to imagine whatsoever you desire, in this moment, it is less fluid to believe whatsoever you wish to believe, here and now. Changing beliefs is a progressive act and should be address right now. Your field of view will always be slightly off from your imagination unless and until you address negative belief systems deeply rooted within you. Thankfully, as you begin to tread the path of imaginal manifestation, you can bypass your beliefs and assumptions about the world on day one — or, rather, on night one.

This moment each night is not only a useful time to imagine your desires, but to restructure your assumptions as well. The more you visualize solutions to your problems, joy in place of despair, and openness in place of frustration, the more your subconscious will begin to align with your desires and your preferred state of being.

Our conscious mind is notorious for reminding us of every reason why a certain happening is impossible. "How could you possibly manifest a beautiful home by the ocean... you're unemployed!" "Obviously your boss will never promote you, he yells at you every day!" We may not speak to ourselves with this type of phraseology, but the feelings with which we blanket ourselves each night are the emotional equivalent of those words. When you make the conscious decision to focus upon only that which makes you joyful each night, only then will your field of view begin to shift in such miraculous ways that will even outstrip your hopes.

Whatsoever you imagine in this hypnotic state will appear in your field of view with exceptional accuracy. Resolve yourself to never focus on anything disastrous or negative during these highly susceptible minutes but choose only to focus of what you wish to deliberately manifest. Watch as your field of view changes drastically and dramatically.

When you begin on the path of using your imagination to manifest your desired field of view, liken the new journey as one beginning in that old, wrecked vehicle. Low tire pressure and a weak engine are the name of the game. Yes, this vehicle is enough to get you all around town — anywhere you choose to go — but the ride won't be as smooth as it could be, and certainly there may be incidents of a flat tire and mechanical problems. As you progress and with practice become more and more effective at properly using your imagination, you will be shifting into better and faster vehicles, and so over time your imaginal acts will be so powerful that you can consider yourself to be driving a supercharged Lamborghini. However, initially, we all typically start out in a slower, bumpier ride. This is because of our rooted beliefs surrounding hardship and worth. However, think about this semi-hypnotic state, which you enter each and every night before sleep, as a time when you can ride around town in a leased Lamborghini — or whatever car you prefer! Each and every night, you are given a leased car to drive, and you can choose to drive anywhere you desire, and only when you make the decision not to drive around in the dangerous part of town — through the neighborhoods of stress, frustration and misfortune — then you will rise to heights only seen in your imagination.

Entering the Hypnotic State

Although we naturally enter the semi-hypnotic state every night, it is very much possible to consciously enter this state whenever we so desire. When we are preparing to fall asleep, there is no conscious process required to enter the semi-hypnotic state, because it happens naturally, with or without our conscious consent. However, there is a specific process that can be used in order to evoke this state of consciousness on demand.

Before delving into the process, it is important to understand what it means to be in a semi-hypnotic state. Before you fall asleep, pay attention to your physical and mental states, and how you subtly descend into stillness. In those last few minutes before falling asleep, your physical body becomes incredibly relaxed. This relaxation is so strong that you almost lose sensation of your limbs. Your awareness recedes into itself, and you lose your focus. On the mental plane, your internal dialogue shuts down, and you move into an imaginal space marked more by visual sensations as opposed to aural self-talk. Finally, without realizing in the exact moment, your consciousness shuts down and you enter the realm of the pure subconscious.

This nightly trance can be likened to a deep meditation, where your focus is projected inwardly, and you become one with your mind. In order to enter this state consciously, you first need to choose one, singular thing you are going to imagine. Know beforehand what you wish to project onto your subconscious and keep it simple. Create the afterthought and go into the semi-hypnotic state with the intention of planting that one and only seed. Then, you are ready. The first step is to enter a state of intense physical relaxation. Simultaneously, you must shut out all distractions, including potential disturbances such as your phone. Your physical posture isn't all that important, as long as you are not driving or operating anything mechanical.

Once you are completely relaxed, with your eyes closed, focus on a singular thing, like counting numbers. The point is not to lull you into sleep, but to situate your mind in a place void of all distractions.

You must temporarily forget about that email you need to send, and anything else that would otherwise occupy your mind.

It becomes easier to let go of all worldly distractions when you affirm to yourself that you are entering this state for only a few minutes. Go into the hypnotic state with that mindset, because your mind will release itself much more easily, knowing that it is only a temporary break. If you go into this meditative state thinking you might persist for a lengthy period of time, your mind will inevitably become impatient.

Once you have relaxed your body and quieted your mind, play the afterthought, which you have already designed, over and over again. Do this for at least a minute, and not exceeding a few minutes. That is enough to plant the seed. While doing so, ensure that your rational mind remains quieted, so as not to disturb your imaginal act with doubt and worry.

Notice that this type of imagining is different from the day to day imaginal acts. With this technique, you are dedicating a time and place to yourself, where you move inward and near the edge of slumber, intentionally. You quiet everything around you and inside of you, and focus on one, specific scene that that you wish to create. As opposed to ordinary imaginal acts, here you are attempting to bypass the wakeful, conscious mind and sow the seeds directly into the garden of your subconscious.

This technique is not meant to be a replacement of the continual use of your imagination, but rather a compliment to it. You must, throughout your day, focus only on proactive and positive imaginal acts, in order to shift your field of view. This technique, however, acts as a powerful complement to your manifesting arsenal. It not only impresses upon your subconscious with far greater efficacy but will increase your confidence in your ability to manifest.

Singular Hypnosis

The importance of focusing on one, singular afterthought cannot be overstated. Throughout the day, we think of countless different words and images. It would be impossible — and inadvisable — to try and train our minds to be hyper-focused all day, every day, as that is not our natural and intended state. However, in order to effectively utilize the immensely powerful time shortly before sleep, we must be laser focused on one issue. You must decide, before going to bed, what it is that you wish to manifest that night, and your scene can be different every night, if you so choose. As long as you have consciously designed your afterthought before entering the semi-hypnotic state and have determined that you will sow that seed into your subconscious, then you will surely use your imagination wisely.

Focusing on too many things before falling asleep will only serve to reawaken your mind, and confuse your subconscious, causing your field of view to be a less accurate representation of what you intended it to be.

Vividness

Just as your regular imaginal acts need to be as realistic as possible, implementing all five senses into your imaginal acts, so too should be your hypnotic visualizations. Without reawakening your conscious mind, incorporate conversations, if relevant. If you want to visualize a promotion at work, part of your visualization might be a conversation you have with your boss, receiving congratulatory words. Remember, in imagining the afterthought, you are imagining a scene which would take place if and only if your desire had already been fulfilled. Any imaginal act which implies means, or something which would happen in the middle, is ineffective at best, and counterproductive at worst. Feel your new office desk, hear the praise from your family, and feel the joy of your new and improved salary. Include as much sensory vividness as possible and imagine from first person point of view. Using the same techniques in these visualizations as you would at any other time of day, create your afterthought to be as lifelike and vivid as possible, and it will shortly appear in your wakeful, physical field of view shortly thereafter.

Early to Bed, Early to Rise

The semi-hypnotic state, occurring in the last moments before slumber overtakes you, is the single most powerful time period for deliberate and constructive manifestation. During this period, you are able to maneuver your present field of view to face any direction you desire, effectively, accurately and speedily. There is, however, another useful time, full of advantages: morning.

Though morning is a highly useful time — and I highly encourage you to make use of it daily — the purpose of early morning visualization is different, and far less hypnotic than the time before sleep.

We've all woken up on the wrong side of the bed, numerous times. And, we all know what follows... Everything seems to go wrong, and you just can't catch a break. From the morning routine, to the commute to work, to the interpersonal engagements throughout the day — it all frustrates. On those days, how good does it feel to finally get home? If it does, it's usually because you spent the day imagining the relief you will find once you return home.

On those days that you wake up on the wrong side of the bed, everything seems to go wrong because whatever feeling you impress upon your subconscious directly upon waking up, will be expressed that very same day, in the form of the overall mood. By mood, I mean both your emotional mood, as well as the mood during the hour-to-hour events that occur. There seems to be a direct correlation between how you spend the first few minutes of your day and how the rest of your day unfolds. By taking control of your thoughts and feelings in the first few minutes that you are awake, you are able to curb a great deal of frustrations that would otherwise be expressed in your field of view that day.

Just as waking up feeling blue, or anxious, causes a chain of reaction for hours to come, so too will that same chain of reaction be influenced when you utilize your free will to consciously impress relaxation into your morning subconscious.

Set the Record Straight

When conducting your morning imaginal acts, it is less important to focus on sensory vividness, and more important to focus on the raw, emotional feeling. In other words, right upon waking up, and in the minutes that follow, your mind is still starting up, and trying to focus on imagining a specific afterthought is not always possible at that early time of day. Instead of trying to force yourself to imagine the scene you wish to manifest in your field of view, focus simply on your feelings. Waking up feeling rushed will ensure a rushed commute. Getting though your morning routine feeling frustrated about having to go to work will create a frustrating day at the office. These moments when you are *turning on* are primal, and raw. You would do well to calm yourself as you run through your morning rituals. As you wash up and brush your teeth, affirm to yourself that you feel okay; that the present moment is pleasant; that today is going to be a calm and peaceful day; that something wonderful will definitely happen to me today. Focus on feeling good, and on letting go of worry, and the rest of your day will follow suit. This activity will prove to be a good lesson on the power of expressing the right emotion. While imagining specific scenes that you want to manifest is integral to the expression of you field of view, releasing negative emotions, and impressing upon your subconscious feelings of calmness and solidity are crucial to how your daily events are colored.

For example, if you work, then you must commute to work. Whether consciously projecting feelings of joy or frustration, either way you will commute. The feelings you impress upon your subconscious, upon waking up, will only color the events of the day which would otherwise happen, regardless.

It is important to utilize your God given free will to set the record straight. You are in control of what occurs in your life, and you are in control of how you will feel when those occurrences show up in your field of view. There is always a time-delay between the imaginal act and the appearance in your field of view, but when operating on the level of feeling, the projections from your subconscious are more immediate. Using the morning to let go of the heaviness we so often carry with us will prove to be an immensely — and immediate — rewarding technique.

The Game (of Life) Plan

The game of life is certainly a complicated one. Although success and achievement are our natural right, that state is often the most difficult for most to materialize. Organization is one of the critical distinctions between success and failure, whether on a school assignment, a work project, or your deliberate decision to manifest your field of view to your liking. Anything conducted in a haphazard fashion will inevitably fail — not because imagination won't become reality if it is done incorrectly — but because the doer will become fatigued and confused over time. Organization is critical to achieving success in this game of life.

On a weekly basis, make a game plan for the following seven days. Set aside various times throughout the day when you will consciously manifest through the mechanism of deliberate imagination. Adopt, as a complement to your morning routine, an additional few minutes to align your mind in a positive state. Make a list of what you hope to manifest — keep the list short at first, and as you gain traction in this endeavor you are encouraged to grow your list. Design your after-thoughts ahead of time, so that when you decide to imagine them, you are more accurate and deliberate.

CHAPTER 7

VIBRATION

"Gratitude is not only the greatest of virtues, but the parent of all others"

—Cicero

Titled *Vibration*, this chapter could have just as accurately been titled *Gratitude*. In most Law of Attraction circles, the idea of raising your vibration is as critical, if not more so, than directing the movie of your life through the power of imagination. Countless videos and books exist, promoting the idea that if you maintain a state of pure joy, only joyful things will be attracted to you. Likewise, wallow in misery and miserable happenings will find a way to you — as the saying goes, misery loves company. While consciously choosing to curate your emotional landscape is never a bad idea, there is a surplus of misinformation about the meaning of raising your vibration, as well as its purpose.

One of the chief misconceptions is that a state of ecstasy must be maintained in perpetuity in order to attract events, people and circumstances which will evoke that same emotion. States of strong emotion are only meant to act as bridges between states of normalcy. For example, were you to win the lottery, a state of unbridled joy would take over and you would become nearly delirious with excitement. That feeling, however enjoyable, will not persist — nor is it meant to. It would be unhealthy to remain in such a hyper-emotional state for an extended period of time. Similarly, when we intend to raise our vibration, we should not strive to maintain such highly charged emotions, because we will always fail in this endeavor. Our biochemical system is not built to handle intense emotion for long periods of time.

In general, however, we should keep our negative emotions in check, and should shy away from reacting impulsively and negatively to every occurrence in our daily life.

Quantum physicists tell us that the material universe we see all around us is an illusion. Everything, they say, is at its core energy vibrating at varying frequencies. The reason a tree is a tree and a stone is a stone is because these energy bodies are vibrating at different frequencies. Simple on its surface, this theory of reality is actually incredibly complex, and it combines science with spirit.

Because we live in a world of vibration, we are attracted to people, places and objects which are compatible with our personal frequency and are put off by those which aren't. Because we are human beings given the gift of free will, our frequency is fluid — that is, changeable. Throughout our lives we are constantly moving up and down in frequency, and our frequency is determined by the thoughts and feelings we impress upon our subconscious. Emotions like love and gratitude resonate on an incredibly high frequency, whereas fear, shame and insecurity operate far down on the frequency spectrum. Whatsoever we imagine, with feeling and conviction, is impressed on our subconscious and in turn our subconscious will resonate to the tune of a certain frequency. At any point in time we can change our frequency by shifting our thoughts and feelings, and this shift will lead to a change in our field of view — for better or for worse.

If every emotion represented a specific room in the castle of your soul, gratitude would be the throne room. The highest of all expressions, gratitude acts as the master key to every solution, desire and path to prosperity afforded to us in this universe. Gratitude is the single most powerful emotion, which raises the frequency on which we resonate higher and faster than every other emotion. Not only is gratitude the single most powerful tool for raising our vibration in frequency, but gratitude also acts as an amplifier, turning our subconscious into a megaphone, blasting positive energy into the ether. The most effective way to raise your vibration, which is an integral part of the process of manifestation, is gratitude.

When steeped in the darkness of tribulation, showing gratitude can be a difficult feat. Not to fear, as there are techniques for overcoming this hurdle.

No book on spirituality would be complete without devoting a section to the blessing of gratitude. Gratitude, and also gratefulness, improve our mood in the present moment, rectify our problems in the immediate future, and unlock every door to unfathomable prosperity in the long term. By showing gratitude for the blessings you currently have, and by waiting in grateful expectancy for your blessings to come, you are literally magnetizing to you every possible pleasurable experience, and opening opportunities that were heretofore closed. God will shower upon you every blessing you have prayed for, and your cup will overflow. Whereas imagination is the key to achieving that which was desired, gratitude is the master key that opens and expands energy for good — both tangible and intangible.

When you show gratitude, sincerely, and with the right attitude, you will experience quantum leaps that are unprecedented in the story of your life. Take the leap of faith, and dive head first in the ocean of gratitude, and watch where the currents of happiness and abundance take you.

You don't need an explanation on how to be grateful. This highest of emotions is built into the fabric of your soul, and its expression is as natural as breathing. Just as we breath consciously and unconsciously; awake and asleep, so too does your soul have the capability to show gratitude endlessly, in all circumstances. When your heart is overwhelmed by the hardships of this world, naturally the light of gratefulness will be diminished, but as you embark on this most power path, expressing the highest emotion of gratitude, you will recover the natural inclination already present within you and gratitude will become a state of being, unceasing.

The more you show gratitude, with sincerity, the more quickly your desires will manifest in your field of view; the more you will experience what you desire; the more consistently you will feel joy; the more your mind and body will heal; the better your life will become, in every aspect of your life. Areas of your life that you have not focused your imagination upon will improve as well, as gratitude is the universal balm, which soothes and heals everything material and non-material in your field of view.

Attitude of Gratitude

It is important to be grateful for whatever you have. It is equally important to be grateful for all that you don't have. Gratitude is the ultimate universal law, more powerful than karma. The reason gratitude is so important is because it encompasses every spiritual virtue in one neat package. Gratefulness in all our daily affairs lends a level of patience in the grateful person, not becoming perturbed by apparent loss or lack, because the grateful person knows that in all things there is room for thanks. The one who is constantly grateful becomes more and more generous toward others, because the confidence in knowing that more will come is always present. The grateful person is courageous in the face of life's difficulties because of the strong and loving connection to Spirit. Gratitude is the unbreakable bond between creature and Creator and expressing thankfulness in all things is the highest form of prayer. This world is imperfect by design, and as such when we show gratitude in all things, we are in one sense letting go of all attachment to our desires. There will **always** be room for more, and our desire nature will ever remain insatiable. Expressing a loving, thankful expression of gratitude sends out every type of positive affirmation and shows God that we are ready to receive more and more.

Developing the attitude of gratitude is not a onetime act, and neither is it something that should be done intentionally during the allotted hours of the day. In the beginning, set time aside to practice gratitude, but over time it must become a way of life. When your subconscious is seated on the throne of gratitude, you are affirming that there is no real lack in the universe — and in your life as well. This belief, or assumption about the world will project untold abundance in your field of view.

Always acknowledge what you already have. Never start from where you wish to be but begin from where are currently are. When you place your focus on what you currently have, with the feeling of joyful thankfulness, you will be given more, and more and more.

No matter what you choose to manifest in your life through your imagination, you will only be as content as you are grateful. Scores of people win the lottery, or receive sudden inheritances from a distant relative, and yet remain as miserable as ever. When you are in a state of ungratefulness in your present circumstances, you will remain so in the face of abundance. Gratitude is directly correlated with joy, and the former always increases the latter. When you are joyfully grateful for what you currently have, no matter how little or how temporary, more will be given to you, and as you linearly increase in gratitude, even more will then be given, evermore.

It is important to show gratitude even for what we don't have. Think about how many times your prayers seemed to go unanswered, and how with the passage of time it was made clear to you that had you received your request, it would have made your life far more difficult. There is no one who prays consistently except that he can attest to this truth. Showing gratitude for what seems like lack is the highest expression of trust in the Divine and shows that we are humble in mind and spirit. The attitude of gratitude is the electric charge that runs through all of our manifestations, and while you manifest whatsoever you imagine, without gratitude, you cannot enjoy your manifestations. Everything you desire will come to you through the proper use of your imagination — yet will fall away from you as quickly as it appeared if you do not make the habit of gratitude a consistent one.

There is no limit to the endless bounty God can and wants to give you. There is a divine purpose to this world, and its intentional imperfection. Showing gratitude in this fallen world is seldom easy in the beginning. However, upon successfully impressing the permanent state of gratitude upon your subconscious, you will never be able to return to your former state. The difference between a life of gratitude and one without is like the difference between night and day. Just as the sun brightens our mood, causes the vegetation on the earth to grow, and beautifies every environment, so too are the effects of gratitude in your life.

It's Magic

Gratitude is truly magical. In fact, when you make gratitude a consistent practice, you will actually begin to see the world as a more magical place. As children, our imaginations were so powerful. The most mundane, humdrum of events could be turned into a chapter in the fairytale of the day. Our minds and souls were fresh, and untainted by the anxieties of the world, and we were able to layer anything we imagined over the world that was our field of view. Gratitude, when done consistently, has a similar effect — it makes your mind more youthful. Showing gratitude consistently creates a mental atmosphere of patience, as sudden inconveniences won't phase you. Once you embed the fertility of gratitude into the garden of your subconscious mind, you will be living on a higher plane, and the toils of this world will lose their hold upon you. Just as the youth are able to stay awake for long hours and expend immense loads of energy while the elderly simply cannot, in the same likeness does gratitude make the spirit more youthful, able to endure with incredible ease the occurrence of misfortunes — and you will be amazed how every misfortune which appears in your life will drop just as suddenly, as your persistent state of gratitude will erase every trace of error.

Just as the morning sun puts out the stars of the heavens, so too will the light of gratitude put out the stars of hardship which have dotted the landscape of your subconscious.

Gratitude is the alchemical principle of life. Although we have not (yet) discovered how to transform lead into gold, we *have* discovered how to transmute poverty into wealth. Countless rags to riches stories have been documented, and the defining commonality that runs through them all is gratefulness during what seemed to be lack, and continued gratefulness as abundance poured in. The great transformational principle of reality is gratitude for all things, people, circumstances, environments, and socioeconomic status. Be grateful for what you currently have, and are, and you will be given more, evermore. Like magic, gratitude is the universal law of increase, of expansion. When you are grateful for the money you have, you will receive more money. When you are grateful for your community, the neighborhood you live in, it will be made more beautiful in your eyes. When you feel gratitude for your body, the highest piece of bio-technology in the history of the universe, you will see it become healthier, more beautiful and more youthful. When you are grateful for your family and friends, no matter how strained those relations may be, they will be mended and strengthened. When you are grateful for your connection to the Divine, that connection will be strengthened and deepened.

Directly tied to the Law of Attraction, the Law of Gratitude magnetizes all that you desire into your life. Whereas the imagination is integral to manifesting specific scenes onto your field of view, gratitude attracts beauty and abundance into your life generally. Whereas you can direct your imagination to manifest one million dollars, gratitude will cause that million dollars to grow, ad infinitum. It is truly magic, the true alchemy sought after by scientists and philosophers for millennia.

Gratitude opens both the heart and mind. New and innovative ideas will flood your mind, and peace will reign in your heart. Gratitude aligns you in a state of harmony with all universal laws and puts you in the flow of the Earth. Without any effort, gratitude allows your subconscious to flow with the currents of the world and the constant daily struggles you have been so accustomed to will vanish.

Gratitude is a Choice

Like deliberately choosing what to imagine, you can also choose what to feel. Albeit more difficult than the former, choosing how you feel is in no way out of your reach, and the way to exercise your ability to be in emotional control is to express gratitude. Maintaining this state consistently will strengthen and stabilize the mind in ways you have yet to comprehend. I am speaking to you not out of thin air, but through personal experience. Gratitude is the single most healing frequency of vibration and penetrates every situation in life. When you show gratitude, your mind and soul will become stronger, and you will soon begin to feel this inner strength in the form of gravitas. You will find yourself becoming less and less swayed by the ups and downs of daily life —that is gravitas, being centered and still in a moving world. Gratitude is the master key.

When we first make the determination to systematically manifest for ourselves, it feels like an uphill road. Truthfully, any time you go against the grain of habit it will feel like a struggle, and the path of manifestation is no different. Acknowledge that on day one it may be difficult to maintain gratitude in all things consistently and allow yourself to fall back as you need to. Over the course of the first few weeks, however, you should begin to see your world beautified in ways you have never noticed before. Once this occurs, you will find your inner self impulsively giving thanks for all that is around you. Choose to be grateful, and then you will *become* a grateful person.

Appreciation

Directly linked to gratitude, appreciation is the catalyst behind gratitude. If gratitude is the noun, or the state of being then appreciation is the verb. Flood your mind with the awareness of what you have and appreciate the present moment, and everything it contains, and all your upcoming present moments will contain more and better. Appreciation transforms gratitude from a mindset to the final state of being, one in which your awareness is constantly searching for more to appreciate. Not only will this transform your field of view, but you yourself will be irrevocably changed. Commit to the act of appreciation and you will become more loved and more worthy of love, and others will love you more and more.

A wonderful practice to be performed each night is to briefly think about five things you appreciated that day. The following night do the same thing, only you are forbidden from repeating anything from the previous night. Keep this practice going night after night, never repeating what you gave thanks for previously. This practice is more difficult than it seems. After a few days, having given thanks for all the things you are already consciously thankful for, you will be compelled to look for things to appreciate throughout the day. This is a wonderfully uplifting exercise and is sure to raise your vibration.

Gratitude in Advance

One of the most powerful tools for achieving that which you desire is to show gratitude for it in advance of receiving it. Though not a difficult task, this method of achievement feels a bit off. When you first do it, it feels a bit funky — like you're knowingly doing something incorrectly. Our natural disposition is to ask, receive and give thanks. We are taught this process from our earliest childhood years. No child is instructed to say thank you before receiving, and as adults it feels very, very strange when doing it for the first time.

When giving thanks before having received anything, we are indicating to our subconscious that we have already received our request. This may seem like a simplistic and downright false notion of our subconscious, which we are oftentimes told is our super-intelligent higher self. Perhaps there is a portion of our subconscious which has access to infinite intelligence, but for all practical purposes here on Earth, our subconscious works in a more robotic, mechanical manner. That which is fostered in the mind is projected in reality. When you say thank you, from the depths of your heart, those words are impressed upon your subconscious much the same as does your imagination, and you will receive all that you have shown gratitude for in your field of view.

In scripture of nearly all traditions, there is the notion that we are to ask the Divine in a state of thankfulness that we have already received. This idea is not limited to Christianity but found in every major word religion. When we petition, through words or imaginal acts, we will inevitably receive all that we have asked, exactly as we believe we will receive it. Ask for a home by the beach while believing you will never receive it, and the two forces will cancel each other out. Have faith that you are given everything you request; that your imagination will be projected outward in your field of view exactly as you assume it will. Examine the Earth and its infinite splendor and give thanks that you live in such a prosperous world.

Showing gratitude for that which you have yet to receive is the surest way to receive, and the best preparation for its arrival. The more grateful you are for a certain request, which has yet to manifest in your field of view, the more you will relish in it once it does. This is universal law and can never be altered.

The greatest preparation for abundance is to be grateful that it is all around you. Then, you will receive it in your hands, able to use it as you wish. When you work in harmony with universal law, which is constant and ever present, every need and desire is effortlessly supplied in ways you cannot currently imagine.

If you decide that you will wait to give thanks, both in words and attitude, until after you have received your request, all you will succeed in achieving is more waiting. Your request will be fully yours in the energetic realm but will not materialize successfully until you offer thanksgiving. The overriding emotion in that scenario is waiting. Focused on the offering of gratitude, your imaginal act would come to pass at blinding speed and fullness.

Stand by your faith, which cannot be diminished in the face of apparent lack and walk in the light of gratitude knowing full well that your requests are already given to you before you even ask, and as you imagine it to be, so will it be, for that is universal law. Express to your subconscious that you already affirm your request's present reality, and it will be your present reality without any doubt. Never hesitate to believe that abundance is already yours, even if you cannot see it. Overcome any obstacles to your belief that everything you desire, ask for, and imagine is yours by right.

One of the reasons why gratitude is so effective when given in advance is because gratitude can be likened to electricity. We are constantly surrounded by abundance, but that prosperity needs the life-giving charge in order for us to access and enjoy it here in the physical. When we develop the habit of thanksgiving for our present moment, and for the imaginative acts we have yet to manifest, we are effectively showering the energetic sphere with bolts of lightning, giving life to our dormant prosperity. If you want to turn your life around, become grateful, and you will be amazed at how your life turns around.

No Work to be Done

It has been mentioned throughout this book that when you decide to manifest something into your field of view, and you do it properly according to the process and techniques outlined, your manifestation will materialize no matter what you do — or don't do.

Raising your vibration is considered canon in many Law of Attraction guides, and while we absolutely do live in a vibratory world, a lot of misconceptions around the topic must be dispelled. Over and over again the reminder is needed: use your imagination properly, and you will manifest that which you have imagined at a certain point in the future. Everything which needs to fall into place in order to make your manifestation a reality will occur in the exact order necessary. Whether you consciously work on raising your vibration or not is mostly irrelevant to creating a specific manifestation. That is not to say that raising your vibration is meaningless — that idea couldn't be further from the truth. As you rise up in frequency, pleasurable happenings occur in your life with greater frequency and stronger intensity. If you operate at a low level of vibration, and you manifest something of high value to you in exactly the proper manner, you can be sure that your manifestation will appear in your field of view. You can also be sure that you will lose what you manifested shortly thereafter, because that object or circumstance of high value to you will be repelled by your low vibratory state. This is one of the numerous reasons why it is so crucial to get in the habit of constant gratitude, and of specifically showing deep gratitude for the blessings which you know are coming but haven't materialized yet.

The idea of raising your vibration is an important one, and although entirely unrelated to manifesting a specific thing or event, it is crucial in maintaining prosperity in your life over the long term.

We've all read stories about someone who wins the lottery and four years later is bankrupt, friendless and homeless. This is a terrible circumstance to experience, but one which was brought about by a profound lack of love, gratitude and faith — the three emotional frequencies which elevate you more than all others.

When you specifically manifest, know that once the seed has been properly planted, and you have followed the guidelines explained in this book, zero conscious effort is required. However, in order to create the lifestyle of prosperity, joy and abundance, you must transform your daily practice of sincere gratitude into an enduring lifelong state of sincere gratitude. Only then will you become a true magnet for joy, wellness, and abundance.

Vibrational Match

One of the oft repeated mantras we hear is that we cannot attract that which doesn't match our vibration. As a vibrational being, you can visualize a certain thing all day long, but if you aren't living a life of 24-hour ecstasy then you're only running a fool's errand. There is absolutely truth in the idea that you should strive to raise your vibration, and that when you do so you will begin to attract immense prosperity into your life — and, you will begin to repel negative and frustrating circumstances. Regarding specific manifestations, your only responsibility is to manifest as outlined earlier in this book, and go with the flow of life and you will be taken where you need to go; others will be taken where they need to be; and the entire world will conspire to bring you to your imaginal act in the flesh.

If a certain vibration is required for you to attract that which you desire, then by fulfilling the imaginal act properly, life will guide you to people and circumstances which will raise your vibration. In order to achieve something specific, you don't need to worry about raising your vibration here and now.

There is another fallacy to the idea that you can only achieve something once you become a vibrational match to it. The fallacy is that we are not capable of staying in an emotionally excited state for long periods of time. Emotions like excitement and ecstasy are only bridges that carry us between long term states of being. This high-level of emotion is transient by nature, and the effort involved in maintaining those states all day, every day is wasted energy. The best emotion to emit that will help you achieve a long-term, high frequency vibration is gratitude, and the higher your vibration the more beautiful your inner and outer worlds become.

Letting go is essential to the game of life. The more you put conscious focus and effort on forcing high vibrational emotions, the more you will tire yourself out and feelings of frustration will inevitably ensue. Commit yourself to manifesting the proper way, place the act of appreciation on a pedestal, with the intention of becoming a permanently grateful person, and let go and embrace the flow of life, and you will be carried by the currents of life to wherever it is you need to be.

Allow your vibrational frequency to shift naturally, and never try to force manic emotions because you think that will somehow prevent disaster from striking. Raising your vibration will not be achieved through short but intense bursts of forced emotion, but rather will result from a lifestyle of thankfulness and a disposition of contented detachment from the outcome.

The World is Your Reflection

There is no separation between you and what you experience in your field of view. The language of "attracting" or "matching" are only used to help get the point across in an easily understandable way. The deeper truth, however, is that whatsoever is contained within the subconscious will be expressed in your field of view. The world is but a mirror reflecting back to your subconscious, and will reveal all that you are, imagine and believe to be. When you raise your vibratory state, you are beautifying your subconscious through various virtues, including gratitude, love and courage. That beautifying and strengthening impression upon your subconscious will be reflected back to you in the form of a more beautiful and pleasurable world around you.

The universe, which is your field of view, will conspire via infinite wisdom and intelligence to manifest whatsoever you determined to manifest. Looking at the world in this light eases the complexities of understanding how manifestation works, and results in a totally inward focus. Rumi, the great Persian poet and mystic, said "yesterday I was clever, so I wanted to change the world. Today I am wise, so I am changing myself." Change yourself, and impress upon your subconscious the highest of vibrations, and you will "attract" to your life every pleasant experience, and all that you deliberately manifest. This "attraction," or drawing out of the universal supply what you imagine is but another way of expressing the same universal truth:

your field of view, and all that is contained within it, is a reflection of your subconscious, which you have the power to influence.

Sincerity

Much needs to be said on the topic of sincerity. We can lie to the world and everyone in it, but we can never lie to ourselves. Our subconscious knows the reality of life better than our conscious minds do, and sincerity is the watchword in the game of life. If your belief in your ability to manifest anything you choose to create is found wanting, then your creative acts will never manifest with true accuracy. In the same light, if you mouth the words of gratitude but inside you feel no sense of appreciation, it is that inner feeling that will win the day. No amount of lip service will alter the reality that your inner voice is creating.

Only when you develop a real sense of joy in the present moment, and a sense of appreciation for all the beauty and abundance around you, will you truly free yourself from the shackles of powerlessness. Gratitude conveyed with genuine sincerity will uplift your vibratory frequency, thus creating all around you a more harmonious environment, and will open you to the power of being natural creators of your field of view. Over time, with sincerity in your joy, you will learn to manifest without inner hesitation, and everything in your environment — including other people — will conspire to bring your desires to pass.

Your subconscious cannot be tricked, and so sincerity is the only way forward. When you give thanks for something, you bless it, and because everything in your environment is a natural projection of your subconscious, you are in turn blessing your own self. Gratitude is a looped system which creates the electric charge necessary for total harmony between the inner and outer worlds.

Whenever you feel dissatisfied, know that those feelings are being expressed with sincerity, and yet negative emotions are only there to compel you to take correct action. Nothing unpleasant exists in your field of view simply due to Divine spite. God is the most loving and the most merciful, and desires only our success. Dwelling on negative emotions — which is always done with sincerity since we would never go against our natural state and *try* to feel bad — is a sure way make the situation worse, because that sincerity coupled with imagination will produce a more unpleasant field of view. Conversely, when you feel satisfied, excited, joyful, serene and powerful over your life, that state of high vibrational frequency will draw to you, and out of you, more feelings of contentment for which to feel sincerely grateful.

Sincerity is like the final stamp upon an emotion. As we mail letters of emotion to our subconscious, continuously, those without the stamp get lost in the mail, and too often it is our positivity that isn't truly sincere, and thus has little to no effect upon our field of view. When you choose gratitude to help create a more harmonious life, you must do it the right way, and that entails only one ingredient — genuine sincerity.

Do not offer the state of gratitude with the intention of getting more. That will inevitably take you down a road of loss, for it wasn't real to begin with. The act of appreciation will ensure that you feel thankfulness for the beauty around you, and that you become thankful because thankfulness is your natural state. For no other reason will you be in a state of gratitude, except that it is your natural, joyful state. Then, and only then, will the entire universe dive into the palms of your hands.

CHAPTER 8

FOOD FOR THOUGHT

"Never finish a negative statement. Reverse it immediately, and wonders will happen in your life"
—Joseph Murphy

At no point during our waking hours can we turn off the inner conversation going on in our mind. Self-talk comes in various forms, but in essence anything which involves hearing words in your mind comprises self-talk. Whether we consciously pay attention to our inner self-talk is irrelevant to its effects upon our subconscious and therefore our field of view. Many self-help gurus have touted the benefits of affirmations, or positive, declarative statements repeated to oneself in order to effect a positive change in the field of view. Positively affirming concise and declarative statements in one's mind is actually less rooted in spirituality and more in psychology. The notion of self-fulfilling prophecy becomes relevant here. A socio-psychological concept, a self-fulfilling prophecy refers to someone predicting — or, expecting — something, and this prediction later becomes true because the person's belief in the prediction will cause subconscious patterns of behavior to emerge which will result in the prophecy's coming to pass. Self-fulfilling prophecies can result in both positive or negative outcomes.

It is important to point out that in the traditional psychological understanding, the idea is not that your belief will be projected onto the screen of space, but rather that the individual, without realizing it, will *behave* in such a way as to produce the consequence of the prediction.

At face value, this idea is similar to — yet clearly distinct from — the theory of imagination outlined in this book. The reality of the matter is that the quality of your subconscious creates the quality of your life, and your conscious mind, through imagination and belief, can change the quality of your subconscious positively or negatively. Though robotic, your subconscious is also stubborn. Everything you impress upon it will in turn change it, yet oftentimes the images and beliefs we choose to impress upon our subconscious must be done in a persistent manner in order to produce results. Affirmations work in much the same way. When uttered sporadically they produce little, if anything. When utilized as a daily practice, affirmations are powerful. As with most techniques used to manifest your reality constructively, affirmations are often misunderstood, and their use frequently turns many people into neurotically wired broken records who impulsively repeat phrases in their head without catalyzing any change in their field of view.

Think of affirmations as a supplement to the mind. Whereas imagination is the diet upon which your subconscious feeds, affirmations are like vitamins that you take in order to enhance an already healthy intake. Repeating affirmations too much, or even too loudly in your mind, will simply result in you becoming neurotic, much the same as you would become unwell if you consumed vitamins in massive doses. Affirmations are a powerful supplement — and just a supplement — to your ability to manifest a beautiful field of view.

The Power of Language

Language is the single most effective tool for influencing other people. It was the great orators of history who influenced civilization, and not composers, artists or architects. Language has the ability to move minds and hearts like no other force in the world. If proper and beautiful use of language can be used to sway untold numbers of people, nations and civilizations, then it will definitely influence your own subconscious in ways you cannot readily fathom.

It is established science that language structures thought. The way we speak shapes the way we think, and when we refine our ability to speak, we in turn refine our ability to think. Imagination is the substance of thought, and language the house in which thought dwells. When we train our minds to think the way great orators speak, we will become great ourselves and our field of view will soon match that greatness. Words matter, and our subconscious consumes everything it hears literally and without interpretation. What you think and the words you say to yourself influence how you feel, how you behave, and how you perceive your field of view. As Sigmund Freud once said: "words have a magical power. They can either bring the greatest happiness or the deepest despair."

Developing the Affirmation

Remember that your subconscious will never interpret what you *mean* to say. Every word and every word sequence are impressed upon your subconscious literally and without question. When developing your affirmations, it is important that they adhere to certain ground rules to enhance their efficacy, accuracy and positivity. Speaking, whether out loud or silently in your own mind, will always become a self-ful-filling prophecy.

Whatsoever you say to yourself will be impressed upon your subconscious and will eventually be projected outward and you will live your words in the flesh. When developing your affirmations, the first step is to know that your affirmations have meaning. Whatever you affirm to yourself will influence your subconscious as well as your conscious mind. Your conscious mind will inevitably be colored by the regular repetition of affirmation, and you must acknowledge this truth before you decide to create personal statements. Once you have fully accepted the principle that your affirmations will change your mind and thus your field of view, you should begin creating the statement or statements. Whether you begin with a single affirmation or multiple is up to you, and as long as you follow this guide you will definitely succeed in creating powerful, self-fulfilling prophecies. The purpose of affirmations is not to create a specific event or physical manifestation, but rather a pattern of repeating events. Remember, affirmations are the supplement and not the three-course meal of your subconscious. Affirmations are powerful tools for creating repeating cycles in your field of view.

Now that you're ready to create your affirmations, start by thinking about what you want to affirm: health, wealth, joy, romance, or all of the above. Ask yourself what sort of cycle do you wish to create. Let's use money as the example, since the desire for a high value bank account is basically universal.

1. <u>Keep your language simple:</u> Remember: **subject — verb — object. Money — comes — to me**. In most cases, you will probably want to add an adjective and an adverb, enhancing the statement into: **subject — verb — adverb — object — adjective. Money — comes — quickly — to me — effortlessly**. This type of statement shows the bare minimum, and while it conveys the basic meaning you wish to impress upon your subconscious, I guarantee you if you repeat this exact phrase over and over again nothing will happen. The reason is because this affirmation hasn't been fully developed to the point where it is effective. If your affirmation is a house, this statement is the concrete foundation. There is much to do before it becomes livable.

2. <u>Keep your language first-person and personal:</u> You are not a robot and your subconscious is not a machine. You are a soul and your subconscious is a universe unto itself. In order for your affirmations to have any power over your subconscious you must make them personal, and first-person. As far as first-person goes, this simply implies not speaking to yourself with the he/she/we/they pronouns. This is likely an obvious point, but a necessary

one to be mentioned. Always speak to yourself using the first-person "I."

Making your affirmations personal entails speaking to yourself the way a lover would speak to his or her beloved. Your affirmations should be soft, meaningful and purposeful. You have lived with your frustrations for a long time, and you know your struggles in a way no one else ever could. When affirming to yourself, you must speak to yourself with complete sympathy, understanding and compassion. You are not affirming to your subconscious the way a teacher affirms to her students. You are reminding your subconscious of what it already knows — that you have the right to every form of prosperity and peace. Speak to your subconscious knowing that you yourself are your subconscious. Utilize emotion in your affirmations, as this will electrify them and bring life to your field of view.

3. <u>Be specific and direct:</u> Affirmations are not poems that you recite, nor are they stories. Affirmations are one-sentence statements that should range from 3-9 words in length. Creating a roundabout way of affirming something by using fancy language and expensive grammar will only serve to be counterproductive. Keep it concise, simple and direct: I am healthy; I am constantly receiving good news; or, I love looking at my bank statement because it is always increasing. These statements are purposeful and to the point. The meaning they convey is not up for interpretation and will be impressed upon the subconscious accurately.

4. <u>Employ emotion:</u> Remember, feeling is electric. Repeating statements like a broken record, no matter how personal and matter of fact, will produce no results. How would you *feel* if your bank account literally got bigger every time you looked at it? How would you *feel* if your affirmations were literally a fact of life in the present moment? To *feel* is to be true and know that it is true. This ties back to Step 2, keeping your affirmations personal. There is nothing more personal than raw emotion and designating this as a distinct step was set out due to the importance of infusing emotion into your affirmations. Say it, and also feel it, and know that it thus already is.

5. <u>I am:</u> The most powerful affirmations are those which contain the words "I am." Entire books have been written on the power of those words, and their importance here cannot be understated. While not always necessary, implementing the words "I am" take your affirmation to the next level. Notice the present tense. You *are*. I *am*. If you affirm to your subconscious that you *will be* rich, you will never be rich because your subconscious will continuously create a field of view which is less than rich, keeping the affirmation of being rich ever in the future tense.

Let's update our **subject** — **verb** — **object** affirmation structure: **I am** — **desire** — **clarity**. For example, **I am** — **rich** — **in passionate love**. In this present moment, I am rich in my romantic relationship with the person I love, rich beyond measure. Embrace the feeling of how it feels to be presently rich beyond measure. The measure of richness is clarified by what type of richness, as money isn't the only form of abundance and wealth. Moreover, love comes in various forms, and passionate love, in this example, is the clear and stated form of wealth you are affirming.

I am — **in love** — **with my soulmate**. This structure of affirmation utilizes the power of "I am" with the reality of the present tense and the clarity of thought. **I am** (personally, right now) **in love** (and thus enjoying the pleasurable experience of being in love) **with my soulmate** (thus my love is reciprocated, and I feel the joy of a mutually fulfilling companionship).

Even if you want to create an affirmation that points toward the future, you can still say it in the present tense. For example: "I am beautifying my field of view each and every day," or, "I am always growing my money." In this way, you are speaking in the present tense yet pointing to the future, so that each day builds upon the last.

6. Speak Positively: Because your subconscious never interprets what you say, but takes every word uttered as immutable fact, you must never, ever use language of negativity. For instance, affirmations of poverty and frustration would sound like this: "I am enjoying a life free from poverty and financial suffocation," or, "I am never irritated by traffic." Your subconscious is not in the

business of interpretation. What you mean to say is that you are living a life without any trace of poverty, but what your subconscious hears are the words "poverty" and "financial suffocation." What you wanted was to feel patient and calm in the face of traffic jams. What you'll get is irritation and more traffic jams.

When you create your statements of affirmation you must always include the language of fullness and not lack; of increase and not decrease; of what you desire and not what you wish to diminish. It all goes back to what sort of mental images are sparked as a result of the affirmation. In the last example, repeating the affirmation "I am never irritated by traffic jams" will only produce mental images of traffic jams.

Your subconscious is as powerful as it is literal. Able to project onto your field of view the entire universe, its power cannot be fully comprehended. Inasmuch as it is powerful, it is also literal, and you must be extraordinarily careful as to what images and words you impress upon it.

7. Practice: As the common saying goes, practice makes perfect. However, practice doesn't actually make perfect — it makes permanent. If you practice something incorrectly for 10,000 hours, you will become a master at doing it incorrectly. Practice makes permanent, so follow the guidelines of this chapter and repeat affirmations that will alter your field of view and beautify your experience in this world.

Try and memorize the various grammatical structures of effective affirmations:

subject — verb — object — (emotion)

subject — verb — adverb — object — adjective — (emotion)

I am — desire — clarity — (emotion)

These three basic sentence structures can be universally applied to any affirmation you so choose to create. Infuse your affirmations with purpose and emotion and apply affirmations to every corner of your life.

Self-Script

Going beyond deliberate affirmations, there is another form of self-talk which is very important to note. Throughout the day we all carry inner conversations with ourselves. Whether that is replaying last conversations or imagining new ones, we are constantly playing out conversations in our minds. These inner scripts are incredibly important to curate, because they will inevitably play out in our field of view in one form or another.

The next time you catch yourself playing out an imaginal conversation, take note of the tone of your inner speech. When, for example, you imagine a conversation with your employer, how are you speaking and how is your boss-in-imagination speaking back to you. Know that this inner script will manifest as an outer script, often times word-for-word and sometimes in tone only. If you are constantly engaging with imaginal arguments with your boss, there is no way you can manifest anything other than an argumentative and overbearing boss in your field of view. As this is a universal principle, the same rule applies to any and all your relationships with other people. Script negativity and you will play the part just as surely as others will in your own personal field of view.

Self-scripting plays another important role in how our world is created. Sometimes our inner conversations aren't directed at others in our imaginal space, but simply at ourselves. All day our minds are talking, and oftentimes we are speaking to our own ears. The way you speak to your self is the way your self will speak to you. The world is a mirror of your subconscious and if you speak harshly to yourself — whether in tone or verbal content — your field of view will interact with you in an equally hostile manner. Curate your inner conversations to those of high quality and gentleness and look with amazement at how your external reality completely changes its tone with you.

The way you speak to yourself is the way yourself will speak to you. Put another way, the way you speak to yourself is how the world will speak to you. Those two sentences mean exactly the same thing and are equally factual.

You Are What You Eat Consume
As the saying goes, you are what you eat. By now you should know that you are also what you think. Delving a bit deeper into that idea, you are also what you consume. Every image you look at, article you

read, song you listen to, and affirmation you repeat becomes a plant in the garden of your life. Those who consume gossip magazines will draw gossip into their lives. It cannot be any other way, because everything we consume filters through our senses, takes residence in our thoughts, and then buries itself in our subconscious. When continued attention is placed upon that consumption, it will continue to grow until it is a towering tree in the garden of your field of view, and will darken your garden with its burdensome shade, or, alternatively brighten your view with its glorious flowers. Those who constantly watch or read motivational biographies of great men and women in history will draw upon that energy of achievement and will manifest like surmountable challenges in their own lives. Those who closely follow astrological influences will feel those influences more strongly than those who do not.

Take note of your favorite playlist. The next time you play your favorite songs, listen to the lyrics and ponder on what the artists actually say. Do most of your songs tell stories of heartbreak and grief? Or, are the lyrics you listen to uplifting? Everything which passes through the filter of our senses occupies our minds, and everything in the mind descends into the subconscious.

Once you begin to clean up your realm of consumption you will be amazed at how much smoother life flows in your favor. With each passing day, your subconscious will be fed less and less of the sensory junk food that is all around us, and with that will come a renewing of your field of view.

CHAPTER 9

FREE WILL

"It is not in the stars to hold our destiny but in ourselves"
—William Shakespeare

The most frequently asked questions on the subject of manifestation relate to free will and destiny. The greatest philosophers and sages, through the annals of history, have sought to answer the tough questions surrounding free will and destiny and how the two complement each other. While incredibly complex in nature, both free will and destiny are always in their proper place, and you have full access to your faculties of free will at all times, without exception. Destiny, while ever-present, takes a backseat to free will. When you plant an imaginal act in the garden of your subconscious, the entire universe conspires to create that reality. If a thousand other people must move in a certain direction in order for your field of view to match the contents of your subconscious, they will be moved — and this will occur in such a way that their free will was not infringed.

One of the reasons why you should never attempt to force the middle, but always and only focus upon the afterthought and show keen faith that your manifestation will come about, is because the sheer intelligence required to manifest even something we would consider small, is so astronomical and mind-boggling that an army of scientists, mathematicians and artists alike could never orchestrate your manifestation the way the universe does every moment of your experience. The infinitely complex interactions between every person, event and circumstance that need to occur in perfect sequence, combined with the mysteries of the free will of others — upon which neither you nor the universe can ever infringe — leave the individual bewildered and humbled. However, this fact of life is actually an immense gift. Were you responsible to orchestrate the construction of your field of view, nothing would get done, because you — and the rest of us — are simply incapable of such an infinitely complex feat.

Everything you manifest, when done properly, will come to pass in your own individual field of view. If your manifestation involves another person, it will still come to pass in a way which does not diminish or negate that person's free will or personal sovereignty. It could happen no other way. Everything impressed upon your subconscious will be made manifest in the flesh. Every human being is sovereign, with the full and unadulterated ability to exercise free will equally. Those two statements are not mutually exclusive, but complementary. It is a mystery that won't — and can't — be explicitly explained in this book, yet much of the idea will be explored in depth.

Through all the complexities of life, two simple truths must shine through: that you have the free will to manifest whatsoever you desire, and when other sovereign beings are conscripted by the universal draft, their free will is in no way invalidated. The seeming paradox is universal law and can never be altered. The other truth is that your gain, when attained through the mechanism of deliberate manifestation, never comes at the loss of another. We do not live in a world of limited supply, and this is not a zero-sum game. Even when your gain *seems* to have coincided with another's loss, you have in no way altered their own individual field of view. Their field of view is their own responsibility, and you cannot manifest the loss of something without their energetic consent.

The Entire Universe Conspires

When you consciously choose to manifest your desires upon the screen of space, a series of events will occur seamlessly, in order to bring about your imaginal acts. This chain reaction will almost never occur in a miraculous fashion. However, every manifestation is miraculous.

Let me explain.

The word *miracle* is defined in the American Heritage Dictionary as "an event that appears inexplicable by laws of nature and so is held to be supernatural in origin or an act of God." Merriam-Webster defines *miracle* as "an extraordinary event in the physical world that surpasses all known human or natural powers and is ascribed to a supernatural cause." The Oxford dictionary has essentially the same definition as Merriam-Webster but ascribes God as the presumed cause of miracles.

When you manifest something, no matter what it is, it will appear in your field of view at a certain point in the future. The way it comes about is completely and entirely out of your control, and yet it will come to you so naturally that whenever a manifestation finally appears, you will be tempted to say that it would have always come to me, regardless of my imaginal acts. This is one of the most spectacular features of our reality — that you can be struggling with a certain circumstance year after year with no visible light at the end of the tunnel, and suddenly after you create a way out of that difficulty using your imagination, your exit will be so smooth and natural that you will actually deny your own power.

It is very important to remember that in nearly every case, your manifested reality will not come about by some extraordinary state of affairs, or a chain of events which boggles the mind and soul. Quite the contrary, you will be amazed at how simple and smooth the path is which leads you from your present reality to your future one.

There is a quote that I love from an old 1990s show called Futurama. In one episode, Bender (one of the main characters who embodies every vice and abrasive manner known to man), finds himself lost in space with no apparent hope of returning home. As Bender drifts through space he meets God, though not realizing it at first. When we find Bender conversing with God he quickly discovers that not only is God completely disinterested in the affairs of people but is also aloof and nonsensical. By the end of the episode, you realize that God had been steadily (and, quite effectively), encouraging Bender to use his own power of will and good cheer toward others to save himself and be returned to Earth. Once Bender puts in the effort, only then does God use His miraculous powers to give Bender that final push needed to return to Earth. All the while God is heard laughing in a loving, compassionate manner. Bender then tells his friends back on earth the tale of his encounter with God and informs us Earthlings that we must do everything we can to better our lives here on earth and spread good will toward all because "you can't count on God for jack!" At the end of the episode, the camera pans back to God who says directly to the viewer: "when you do things right, people won't be sure you've done anything at all."

Let me repeat that quote: "when you do things right, people won't be sure you've done anything at all."

When you manifest something right, you won't know you've done anything at all, due to the simplicity of its coming about. You will be astonished at how frequently you are tempted to deny your own power, because nearly every manifestation will come to you seamlessly and so easily, to the degree that you won't believe it could have ever missed you, regardless of your imaginal actions.

One of the core concepts to be learned is that other people will be included in that chain of events which so smoothly unfold. Remember, the fact that other people will be compelled to play their part in the fulfillment of your imaginal acts does not mean that their free will is impinged. This is a mystery and a seeming paradox, yet it is the truth nonetheless. You, yourself have played your part in literally countless manifestations directed by others, and others have played their part in your manifestations. We are all connected at our deep, spiritual core, and we all aid each other in the fulfillment of our desires. If your manifestation requires a single person to aid you, that person will be drawn to you in perfect order, and if your manifestation takes a thousand people, or ten thousand, they will all play their part in perfectly orchestrated order.

Recall that you are not emanating beams of energy from your head and attracting to your field of view that which you desire (or dislike). Your subconscious is actually projecting your field of view onto the screen of space. This is not to say that another being doesn't truly exist outside your reality — each person is a sovereign individual. However, our field of view is our own responsibility, and when we imagine something, it will appear to us even if its occurrence requires others to achieve its fulfillment.

Our manifestation will almost never occur in ways that seem to defy logic, or the natural order of the day. Our manifestations will be projected onto our field of view after a necessary and seamless chain of events occurs, bringing our present field of view to our newly created one.

Just as you should never — and, can never — force a situation to come about without ensuring its delay, you are also unable to compel others to play their part in your manifestation. By imagining your afterthought properly, letting it go and knowing with absolute surety that it is already yours and will appear in your field of view in due course, you have done all you need to do. That's it. Rid yourself of the notion that you need to consciously exert effort, or somehow co-erce other people into certain actions. The universe **and every-thing in it** will conspire to fulfill your manifestation by means of the simplest and most direct chain of events. Your job is not to determine how it will come about, how long it will take, or even who must be involved for its fulfillment — leave that to the universe whose opera-tion is beyond comprehension.

Manifesting Another Person

This book is not a manifesto on casting love spells. There is no magic here, although at times manifesting will *feel* like magic. The fact that every individual is a sovereign entity with free will and control over his or her destiny is not contradictory to the fact that you — and everyone else — is able to manifest your own destiny. Your subcon-scious projects itself outward upon your field of view, as does every-one else's, and the interaction between us all is seamless and perfect.

There are two schools of thought on manifesting romance. The first is that, assuming you want to get together (or back together) with a specific person, you can manifest a relationship with that specific in-dividual, and it will surely come to pass. The other school of thought is that while you can certainly hope to get together with that person, your manifestation may or may not bring you to that specific rela-tionship. You might lose interest and meet another person who fulfills the physical, emotional and spiritual qualifications pertaining to your imagination. In other words, a) you can manifest being with a specific person, or b) you can try but if your imaginal act dictates a certain degree of happiness that only another person can give you, you will manifest that other person. Let's take a look at the first idea.

No matter what you imagine to be true, will be true in your individual field of view. Although your experience of this world, or your field of view, is a projection of your subconscious, the existence of other people is not negated. They exist just as much as you do and are in your field of view — or not — because they are included in your subconscious reality. When you imagine that you are together with someone specific in a serious relationship, they will find themselves inexorably drawn to you. Events will conspire in such a way that you will cross paths with that person, and he or she will see you in a beautiful light. At least, this is the worldview of this school of thought. Somehow or another, the universe will bring you together through subtle forces and you will find yourself one day together with that person. It needs to be mentioned again that other peoples' free will is never negated because of what you choose to manifest. Moreover, whosoever gains or loses something in the process of **your** manifestation coming to pass only gained or lost because of the contents of their own subconscious. When you project a certain reality onto your field of experience, events will conspire to bring that event into being, and whatsoever happens along the way is not in your hands, and you are not responsible for how the chain of events plays out.

Looking to the alternative school of thought, that worldview dictates that you should not focus your manifestation on a specific person, because that in and of itself is meddling in the middle. In other

136

words, if you want a committed and fulfilling relationship, make sure that those feelings are embedded into your intended manifestation, and the right person to fill the role will inevitably come into your life. This may be difficult if a person has such a strong emotional attachment to another specific person, but according to this notion, dictating *who* it is that will give you a fulfilling relationship is telling the universe how to operate. Focus only upon the fulfilling relationship and the best person for the job will be hired! If you are so sure, beyond any shadow of doubt, that only that one specific person can really do the job, then rest assured he or she will come [back] into your life. In either case, you must go beyond the simple imaginal act and employ the power of faith and release, as described in previous chapters.

Finally, and as mentioned multiple times, neither you nor the rest of us have the power to coerce another to the point of invalidating their free will. Our field of view is the projection of our own individual subconscious. Other people who are free agents will be moved in ways known or unknown to them, to fulfill your creative imagination, and meddling in the middle is not your responsibility. When others are influenced by forces beyond us, it is only because their subconscious was in perfect alignment with those forces, and thus were called upon by the workings of the universe to fulfill your imaginal acts.

Destiny

Many people believe that their entire lives are scripted before their birth. Every moment, occurrence, gain, loss and word uttered is part of a Divinely written plan that is unchangeable. Others believe that while pre-destiny is the name of the game, the book of our lives is wholly alterable according to our thoughts, prayers, actions and of course, free will which God has determined not to stifle or interfere with. Still others believe that there are karmic forces at play, and all that we experience is a result of all that we have done either in past lives or previously in this life, or both.

It's been mentioned before and it should be mentioned again: like all things in life, the answer is usually much simpler than we think.

The truth of the matter is, I don't know everything, and neither do you. The truth lies somewhere in the middle, goes the common expression, and it likely applies here. As long as we are here on earth, in this physical dimension having a spiritual-physical experience, it is best not to bother with questions we know can never be answered so long as we are alive. The best way to live your life to its fullest is to always be practical in your approach. It is clear beyond doubt that your imagination, when used properly, will alter your experience here on Earth. That is universal law and is obvious to those who have seen the principle in action. Given that one universal law can never contradict another, the questions surrounding karma, destiny, fate and free will are useful to understand to an extent, and then let go.

Know that you are able to improve or diminish your experience based on the contents impressed upon your subconscious, and in no way are you altering your destiny. Everything goes according to Divine plan, and that includes all the times we use our God-given free will to exercise our imagination and beautify our field of view. We are not helpless and powerless to forces unseen, nor are we left all alone to fend for ourselves. We are placed in a benevolent universe, and given the power to manifest whatsoever we choose, and all of this falls under the blanket of the Divine plan. There are no contradictions to universal law, and you are a free agent.

Vice

Parallel to the idea of karma, what you plant in the garden of your subconscious will sprout into your field of view. Parallel, too, to the idea that what you consume you become, so too do you become that which you project.

When you are happy — genuinely, sincerely happy — for the blessings other people experience, your subconscious will begin to project those experiences onto your individual field of view. When you allow thoughts of envy, jealousy and malice to be projected onto others as a result of what they have, your subconscious will understand that to mean that you despise those blessings and will forbid them from entering your field of view.

You must not only watch what you consume, but what you project as well. Your field of view is a mirror of your subconscious, and people are a mirror to each other. Become genuinely happy when another person gains a new blessing, and increases in a blessing already had, and be sure blessings will enter your life and increase you in joy to the same degree that you felt joy for others.

So often we see what others have but not what they lost. Especially in the age of social media, we only see the good and never the tragic. Know that every single individual, without exception, has talents and weaknesses; blessings and hardships; riches and lack; happiness and sadness. Part of the experience of planet Earth is that we must experience both ups and downs, and we must learn that we, ourselves, are empowered. This is a difficult lesson, one which usually — and paradoxically — comes after long periods of powerlessness. You have free will and the ability to select what enters your field of view, as does everyone else.

Envy burns, just as fire burns. Jealousy is a stranglehold on everything good, and ill-will toward others is poison with which you season your own meal. Gratitude cleanses, happiness brightens, and peace liberates. Express these emotions on behalf of other people, and you will receive that which brings these emotions into your own heart.

Alchemy

Everything you think, feel and believe to be true creates a chain reaction in the unseen realm, which in turn brings about tangible changes in your field of view. Everything in the universe resonates according to a certain vibration, and because you are given the gift of free will you have the unique ability to change your state of vibration. Everything in the universe was created to your benefit, and you have the power to transform every lead casing around the circumstances of your life into bricks of gold and silver. You are given free will, which is both a gift and responsibility. When you show sincere gratitude for your present moment, your present moment will grow exceedingly brighter by the day. Gratitude is the great enhancer, and the spark of life to your imaginal acts. The choice is yours to mold your life as you choose.

When your imagination is impressed upon your subconscious, the entire world conspires to bring about your manifestation. You need not have any fear or doubt as to the manifestation of your imagination because everything in the universe is connected, and whatsoever is the simplest path to the fruition of your field of view — that is the path your subconscious will tread. Big or small; positive or negative; deserving or undeserving; these are terms relative to us and not to the greater forces at play. We impose concepts of big and small; our own understanding imposes concepts of positive and negative; culture and society impose concepts of deserving and undeserving. You need not waver in the face of these conceptual challenges, because whatsoever you impress upon your subconscious, through the process of alchemical imagination, will be expressed in your field of view. This is universal law and cannot be any other way.

The power of imaginal alchemy is yours by birthright. There is no desire too grand, no obstacle too great and no state of being too bountiful so as to be out of reach. Within you is the entire universe. The process of changing your reality by way of imaginal alchemy is far simpler than it appears, and with practice it will become second nature. Just as the health-conscious individual watches his or her nutritive intake, so too must you maintain constant vigilance around what you consume, and what you dwell upon. When you begin to impress upon your subconscious the seeds of a more perfect field of view, you will be amazed at the shifts that take place thereafter. Take mastery over your life and release attachment to everything that has occurred — or not occurred — in the past and let go of your fears around the future. The only thing which truly exists is the present moment, the eternal now, and you have the power.

CHAPTER 10

QUESTIONS & ANSWERS

"Life is not measured by the number of breaths we take, but by the moments that take our breath away"

—Maya Angelou

Do we attract, or do we project? You've used both ideas interchangeably, but they seem like distinct interpretations of how our manifestations come to us.

You are not attracting something to you which is out there in the ether, due to the magnetic quality of your thoughts. Everything upon which you dwell is planted in the fertile farmland of your subconscious and will eventually be revealed in your field of view.

The concept of attracting things to you, hence *Law of Attraction*, essentially outlines an identical flow chart — that your mind and heart, working in sync with each other, have the ability to bring or remove things from your life. What begins in your inner being is then materialized outside of you.

It is less important to debate over the nature of reality — whether your subconscious projects outward or your thoughts magnetize things from out in the universe — and more important to learn how to effectively and properly use your mind to create a life worth living.

I've been really, really negative for a long time. I see that I've been misusing the power of my imagination for years. How long will it take to clear through those years of negativity?

Not that long. If you've been a hyper-positive person for years but for one reason or another dwell upon negativity consistently, it won't take that long for your life to take a downturn. The same rule applies in reverse. No matter how long you have focused on the negative, once you make the determination to use the power of your mind and show gratitude in all things, your field of view will begin to change in the near future.

There is no exact time frame, but typically 90 days or less is the time frame that you will see a marked and obvious improvement to your field of view.

On the topic of timing, how long will my specific manifestation take to come to pass?

There is no set answer here. A manifestation, which was properly impressed upon your subconscious, can take literally seconds to appear in your field of view, while an equally strong impression can take years to appear. It all depends. Remember, things will almost never appear in your life miraculously. There is a natural order to the world, and in the overwhelming number of cases that natural order will be respected.

How long it takes for a specific thing, event or circumstance to come to pass is entirely out of your hands. The operational genius that is your subconscious, your universe, will ensure that your manifestation is materialized according to the simplest and most natural means. There will be a chain of events which lead to the fulfillment of your imaginal act. *How* it happens, and *how long* it takes, is up to the universe and not for you to force.

I've followed every technique in this book because I am determined to manifest a specific thing. However, I'm having trouble "feeling" it. Did I do everything properly? How do I know that I've done it all right?

You will know that you've manifested properly when you no longer feel the intensity of longing. You will know that your desire is already there in the unseen and will appear in your field of view at a certain point in the future.

Think back to a time when you wanted something dearly and received it. How did you feel when you first received it? It was likely a combination of excitement, joy and fulfillment. Longing for a specific desire is a form of hunger, and hunger is pain which results from inner emptiness.

When you received that which you longed for, that hunger was satiated, and the feeling of emptiness was no longer there. In the same way, when you have planted the imaginal scene into your subconscious, believed it to be true and released it to more capable hands, you should feel that inner fullness, or peace, that your desire is there, for you and no one else, and it will materialize soon.

No longer feeling that emptiness is a sure sign that you have manifested correctly. This does **not** mean that you no longer hold the desire in your heart.

Take this example: Say you suddenly lost all of your money and you now have not one dollar to your name. You are days away from being evicted from your home. Now, imagine you received a letter from the bank that by some miraculous happenstance a distant relative passed away and has left ten million dollars in your name, but you must wait two weeks to collect.

Do you think you would feel that intense longing for money, as you had been feeling in weeks prior after losing every cent you had ever earned? Absolutely not — you would be calm, collected, and grounded in the joy that you are [about to be] incredibly rich. Do you think that because you now **know** without any doubt that ten million dollars will be in your bank account in two weeks that you would suddenly lose all desire for money? No way! You would have lost that restless, empty, painful longing for what you so desire while at the same time retaining your desire for that thing, and you will feel joyful and full when you receive your desire in the material sense.

When you enter that middle, balanced state of mind, know that your imaginal act will definitely come to pass, and you can wholeheartedly release it to more capable hands.

How many times should I engage in the imaginal act? Is once enough, or should I keep imagining it until it becomes real in the material world?

In theory, a single imaginal act done properly is enough. Only one time is enough to ensure the manifestation of whatsoever you imagined. This is why so many fleeting thoughts come to pass so often.

The main issue is in the letting go. Fleeting thoughts so often come to pass because they are so effectively let go. We literally think them and then forget about it. There is no intense longing which suffocates those fleeting thoughts, and thus they quickly grow. However, because they were not sufficiently imagined with all the vividness required of a real manifesting act, those fleeting thoughts manifest as fleeting incidents. For example, a memory of a childhood cartoon comes to mind, and then you see a graffiti image of that cartoon while driving under a bridge. This event has no real impact on your life because the thought itself had no real impact on your subconscious. It was a floating seed that happened to be planted.

When you deliberately and seriously manifest something using the full power of your imagination, even if done only once, it will come to pass with as much weight in your life as it had in your imagination.

If you are able to vividly imagine, in first-person, believe it true and sincerely let it go, it will occur in your field of view. If it takes a week or two of consistent imagination to make you *feel* that now it will definitely happen, then two weeks is how long you should imagine it. However long it takes for you to correctly proceed through the manifesting process is however long you should imagine it. If there comes a point where if you are still unable to let it go because you think that you haven't imagined enough, then you must deliberately let it go. The process of manifestation requires no forced effort.

Allow yourself to feel the fulfillment in spirit and then let it go, and you will be fulfilled in the material. If a single imaginal act was sufficient for you to complete the process, then once is enough. If you require a few more times, then go ahead and continue to imagine your afterthought.

Let's say I want to manifest a new home. Should I create one afterthought, or should I enter the imaginal plane with numerous, pre-planned afterthoughts?

To be absolutely clear, you must never imagine anything you think will take place in order for your desire to materialize. For example, if you want to be admitted into a certain master's program, never visualize yourself writing your essays or submitting the application. Just imagine yourself already there at the school, as a student. That is known as the afterthought, or the imaginal scene which embodies all that would happen *after* your manifestation has already come to pass.

When you decide to manifest something specific, in this case a new house, make sure you imagine only the afterthought — a scene which would take place if and only if you lived in your new home. The way you pump life into your imaginal acts is to feel as if you were really there, right now. Feel it so vividly that you forget you are only imagining it.

During the multiple times you imagine your afterthought, it doesn't matter if you imagine the exact same scene each time, or multiple scenes so long as they are all afterthoughts and not process, or middle thoughts. If you can achieve that same level of emotional sensation and sensory vividness in replaying the same afterthought, then keep at it. If you feel that you are imagining more strongly when you diversify your imaginal scenes, then do that.

I know what I want, but I can't really come up with a scene that implies I have it. How do I visualize something when I don't know exactly how it looks when it's all said and done?

This one is a tricky predicament, for sure. We've all experienced it at some point or another. You know exactly what you want — let's say a new job that you're passionate about and that pays well — but you have no idea what that job would actually look like. You don't know what the new office would look like, and you don't know what the job duties would entail. You just know that you want an emotionally fulfilling career that pays really well.

When you come to this stumbling block, the key is to reduce the idea to its simplest components — the senses. If you don't know what your new situation *looks* like, ask yourself what it *sounds* like. Devise a short, concise imaginal conversation with a loved one around the topic of having started a new job. You would likely tell your loved one how happy you are that you're finally in a place in your career that fulfills both your heart and your bank account. What would a conversation like that sound like, keeping the achievement of your job in the past or present tense, since you only imagine the afterthoughts. Never talk about that job you're "going to get."

If you still can't come up with an appropriate afterthought, shift senses. How would receiving that new job *feel* like? Feel the pen in your hands, and the dryness of the paper contract you just signed.

Go through each sense and determine which one feels most relevant to your imaginal scene. If you still can't come up with an appropriate afterthought, then default to the emotional level. Imagine yourself at your current job but with a huge smile on your face, and **feel** the joy, even if you know you won't feel any real joy in your current environment. Show gratitude for your current salary and work environment, even if it seems difficult to do so. When operating on the emotional level, the manifestations which result are usually more general rather than specific, but gratitude is a wonderful starting point if you are unable to create an afterthought. When you show gratitude, and visualize positive emotions, you will be brought to a place that will return those positive vibrations back to you, and if the only way for you to ever feel happiness is away from your current career, then you will be brought to that manifestation.

Do I need to raise my vibration in order to receive my desires?

What you need to do is imagine your desire in the form of its appropriate afterthought and go through the requisite steps outlined in this book. Everything in the middle — the natural sequence of events that brings you from your present reality to your future, manifested one — will occur seamlessly and will be orchestrated by your subconscious. If the raising of your vibration is truly necessary to achieve that which you desire, then your vibration will rise. Everything other than the appearance of your desire on your field of view is considered the middle.

Whatever needs to happen in the middle will happen, and whatever work you need to do will be inspired work, and not effort. You do not need to forcefully raise your vibration because you believe that will quicken the results. Your manifestation will appear as per the natural order of things.

What's the purpose of raising my vibration, then?

You, and everything else in this universe is energy, and everything vibrates at a certain frequency. As human beings, we can move up or down on the vibrational spectrum, and typically we do so by way of our emotional state. The emotional spectrum ranges from love to fear, and everything else is somewhere in between, with gratitude being the crown of emotion, the one which purifies all others. When you raise your vibration by focusing on emotions like love, joy, gratitude and serenity, you are beautifying your field of view. Difficult situations which plague your experience will begin to fade away, and pleasant situations will appear. Pleasant circumstances which are already present in your field of view will be made even more pleasant.

The purpose of raising your vibration is not to "match" the vibration of your specific desire, as you would have no way of measuring your specific vibration anyway. Imagine it and it will manifest. Raising your vibration is a tool to ease your life in a general sense, and to beautify it.

The other effect of having a high vibratory frequency is that the good which you manifest in your life will remain in your life, whereas if you are constantly focused on all things negative and never appreciative what you have, then when you manifest something valuable to you through the power of your imagination, it will appear and disappear in due time, because you have not strengthened it by way of love, gratitude and appreciation.

How accurate do my visualizations need to be? Can I manifest abundance in a more general sense?

It is incredibly important to be accurate in what you impress upon your subconscious. Whereas you can certainly improve the conditions of your life by generally raising your vibration, in order to effectively manifest that which you truly desire you must be accurate in your imaginal acts. Before you begin consciously impressing your subconscious, develop a concise scene & afterthought. Go into your imaginal act with a game plan and a script, and pinpoint with as much specificity as you can that which you intend to manifest. Remember, your subconscious will not fill in the gaps and attempt to figure out what you really meant to manifest. Your subconscious will express that which was impressed upon it — nothing more and nothing less.

Thinking generally about abundance and good fortune is a great habit to develop and it will definitely be expressed in your field of view. However, the magic will only begin to happen when you start impressing specific, definitive and accurate scenes upon your subconscious. Determine what it is that you wish to manifest, create the afterthought which implies that you have already received **exactly** what you want to manifest, and then impress that afterthought upon your subconscious — be definite and do not waver.

What about prayer?

Prayer is an incredibly powerful tool that connects us to God and God to us. Prayer can be performed via words, feelings, and even through exhibiting hope, trust and expectation. When you whole-heartedly believe that God is the most generous, and you know without a doubt that God will enable you to achieve anything you desire, and you walk through life with that expectancy and trust in Him, that is a form of prayer, and God will reciprocate. God never lets any of His creation down.

Prayer, in the context of manifestation, will deepen your faith, belief and expectancy, and will aid you in the process of letting go. While imagining is the first step in the process, belief and release are the other two, and prayer aids both those steps.

Prayer creates and maintains a connection with the Divine that can never be broken.

What is the difference between work and effort?

First of all, work on your part will *sometimes* be necessary for your manifestation to materialize whereas effort is never necessary. At best, effort will do nothing; usually, it will delay or even diminish your manifestation.

When we imagine something, regardless of the supposed impossibility of it, it will happen according to the laws of nature, and the natural order of our world. Sometimes, you will feel inspired to take a certain course of action. This action that you take isn't effort, because you didn't consciously plan it out, thinking that it will help the manifestation come to pass. There is no struggle and the idea to do a certain thing simply came into your mind at the right place and the right time. When that happens, go for it, and rejoice that your manifestation is on its way to your field of view.

Effort, on the other hand, is forced, and it often comes with worry or confusion. Effort is trying to force a situation into being rather that allowing it to materialize.

Work isn't necessary every single time — for example those fleeting thoughts that come to pass. The same may apply to more deliberate manifestations, where it simply comes to pass. Or, work may be required. You simply have to go with the flow of life and follow your intuition at all times. Effort, on the other hand, is never required and usually detrimental to your field of view.

***I'm in a terrible mood today and I can't help it. Usually I'm
able to cheer myself up, but not today. How bad is this for
my field of view?***

Not that bad, I assure you. Unlike many Law of Attraction practitioners who ascribe to the vibrational theory of manifestation, I don't
find it too detrimental to have a bad day. I don't even think it's that
detrimental to your progress if you have a few bad days in a row. It
happens, and the idea that we must always force high vibration emotions down our chakras is unrealistic at best, and harmful at worst.

We're all human beings, and it's okay when we have a really bad day,
or a really bad couple of days. I would caution at allowing that mood
to become a personality trait, however. If you find yourself wallowing
in that negatively for more than a couple days in a row, three at the
absolute most, then it isn't a bad mood anymore, but rather it is becoming a lifestyle.

In terms of your manifestation, being in a bad mood today where
you just cannot uplift your state of mind no matter what, is not a big
deal. Relax, and allow your mind and soul to process those emotions
in a healthy and appropriate manner. When you feel better — and
you will — go back to your practice of gratitude and deliberate manifestation.

How do I counteract those really bad days when it's just too much?

Continuing from the previous question, when you're having one of those days when you are under tremendous pressure, allow it to happen during the day and evening. However, before you go to sleep, use that time of hypnotic imagination to visualize your happy place.

These last few minutes of your day, when used properly, will ensure that the following day is one where your mood has been completely reset. Don't — under any circumstances, no matter how bad you feel — allow yourself to wallow in negativity during the time of hypnotic imagination. We all have those days, and it's okay, but use the last few minutes before sleep wisely, and it will make a world of difference.

What about astrology?

The heavens have their effect on us down here on Earth, but their influence is subtle, and usually acts in a general way. The stars don't cause misfortune or prosperity — they only act as subtle influences. Rise above the astrological plane and use your imagination. Don't just be the main character of your life — be the director! Astrology has its place, and its effects on us, but it is mild, and subtle, and never to be used as an excuse for misfortune.

You are that which you consume, and you manifest that which you expect. If you read your horoscope and believe it will definitely come to pass, then the stars will hold greater sway over your life, because your subconscious invites that energy into it.

I know that I'm not in a great place in life, but I don't know what I want. I'm worried that if I focus on manifesting something specific, and I get it, it will actually backfire and make me more unhappy. How do I know what I should manifest, and how do I assure that my manifestations will bring my joy?

Put your focus on the path of gratitude, and life will open up. When you know that you're currently unhappy, but you genuinely don't know what will make you happy, focus on gratitude. Perhaps manifesting a new house won't bring you any joy, only more bills. Perhaps manifesting a wedding ring on your finger will bring you to the wrong spouse, leaving you wishing you were single again.

These are all real thoughts we have especially when we first embark on this journey. If that's the case, focus on gratitude. Know that your intuition will be opened, and you will discover that which will make you happy, and then you can manifest it.

When you deliberately manifest something, and simultaneously irrigate it with the water of gratitude, it will never bring new problems. That manifestation will only be a joy for you, because you manifested it with the infusion of gratitude. That is the power of gratitude, for it opens every locked door, dispels every difficulty, beautifies everything in your field of view, and increases you in joy and fulfillment.

When you don't know what you want, show gratitude for what you have. The rest will follow.

What do you mean, "imagine in first-person?"

This is critical to imagining correctly. When you construct a scene in your imagination, ensure that your viewpoint is the same as your viewpoint in normal, waking life. In real life, you see through your eyes. Design your afterthoughts with that same perspective.

The purpose is to ensure that your imaginal acts are manifested with accuracy. You will receive what you imagined exactly as you imagined it. If you, in your imaginal scene, see yourself at a distance, in third-person, looking down at the wedding ring on your finger, you might just manifest you, in real life, looking at someone observing their own wedding ring!

The subconscious does not interpret — it only follows orders!

I'm having trouble holding the mental image in my head when I try to visualize in first-person. It doesn't feel natural to me. Why is it so important to imagine in first-person and how can I get better at it?

The importance of visualizing in first-person point of view cannot be overstated. In many cases this is the difference between failure and success, as manifesting in first-person point of view ensures that what is eventually projected onto your field of view is an accurate representation of what you impressed upon your subconscious. When you visualize in third-person point of view, you are drastically reducing the accuracy of your eventual projections upon reality. Imagining the right way will produce the results you desire.

Visualizing in first-person point of view is difficult for most, especially when you first begin doing it. It is not the natural way of imagining for most people, and so holding the mental image in place becomes difficult. Oftentimes the imaginer will revert to the third-person perspective orientation of visualizing. The way to overcome this hurdle is to imagine something you are very familiar with, like your hand. Picture your hand in your mind's eye with as much detail as you can possibly create. Every wrinkle and line, the tone, texture and color; the beauty mark and the hair. Picture it all in your mind's eye. Remember, don't see yourself looking down at your hand — just visualize your hand and nothing else. That is visualizing in first-person, because what you are seeing in your imagination is exactly what you would see if you were to open your eyes right now and look upon your hand.

Hold this mental image for up to a minute, and then using your mind's eye move your focus to your wrist, then forearm. Visualize those body parts with as much detail as you can.

Doing this exercise will train your mind's eye to visualize in first-person. It's easier to visualize your own hand and arm because when our eyes are open, we see them so often throughout the day. Once your mind becomes stronger and more comfortable in this new perspective, you should have a much easier time imagining your after-thoughts in first-person perspective.

Do big things take longer than little things?

It depends. If you believe something must take longer, then it will. For example, if you manifest a barbecue at a gorgeous lake house, and that comes to pass in a week or two, why should it be any different to manifest owning a lake house? Well, there are a few reasons why the latter might take longer. And, there are reasons why it doesn't have to.

If you believe that becoming a homeowner — and of a luxury lake home no less — will take time and hard work, then that will be the probable process: one of time and work. If, however, you believe that your lake house will come to pass no matter what then it will take far less time. Another determining factor is where you currently are in your field of view. If you are currently broke and unemployed, then you may have to wait a while.

Because everything manifests according to the natural order, sometimes many events will have to take place for your imagination to become real. It all depends on your situation, and the power of your faith.

The universe has produced heavenly bodies of such unfathomable proportions, that the range from small to big, as conceived by humans, is so minuscule that in effect there is no difference. As far has the universe is concerned, a pebble and a mansion are the same size; a friendship and a marriage are of the same magnitude.

Can my imagination be utilized to heal my body?

Yes, absolutely. There are numerous and well documented cases of people who have healed themselves using the power of the mind. Your health and bodily functions are considered part of your field of view. Keep in mind, however, that you are not exempt from the natural order of things, no matter how well you use your powers of imagination. No matter how much you imagine it, you are never going to sprout wings and fly, because that is not something humans are capable of doing — it just isn't in our DNA. You can heal your body but cannot affect it in such a way that it defies universal law or the laws of physics.

I imagined my desire perfectly, and followed every step in this book, but what I got was a kind of halfway version of my desire. What gives?

When we imagine something and expect it to be projected onto our field of view, oftentimes we will be shown previews of it — coming attractions, if you will. This is a sure sign that you are soon to receive what you manifested, and it is **not** a sign that you manifested your desire incorrectly, or partially.

For example, let's say you envisioned your new home by the beach, and a few weeks later you are suddenly invited to a beach trip and spontaneously go on a vacation. The place you stay at is an AirBnb, with a balcony overlooking crystal blue waters just as you imagined. This is not the finale of your manifestation, but a coming attraction.

Usually when you are shown these types of coming attractions, it is not only an indicator that your manifestation is surely on the way, but also that it will take some time. How much time is not something anyone can answer, but the moment you think that you have received your manifestation but are disappointed that it seems like a halfway version, rejoice because your imagination is going to be displayed before you in your field of view, in due time.

I want something that another person desires, and there is only one of that thing. If I consciously manifest it, am I taking it away from the other person?

A great example is the job promotion situation. Two people want it but only one can achieve it. First of all, the fact that there is an apparent competition is because that feeling arose out of your subconscious. Theoretically, a promotion could have opened up that could only be filled by you, and no other. However, this promotion opened up and now there is a competition.

Look inward and dispel any feelings of resentment you may have regarding work, and let it go. When you consciously manifest a promotion the right way, you will receive it and any other potential "losers," and by that, I mean people who lost out on the promotion, will be given something else, because you will have erased the notion of competition from your field of view.

Clean up that which you consume, project and believe and all will be made orderly once again. There doesn't need to be winners and losers, but sometimes that is the case because we are inwardly flawed, and we project that scenario outward.

What I'm asking for is <u>seriously</u> big. Realistically, what are my chances?

Exactly the same as your chances of manifesting a cup of coffee. As long as you imagine it properly, and as long as it is physically possible and doesn't deviate from natural law (you can't manifest wings sprouting from your back so you can fly), you can achieve it without any effort. Perfecting your imaginal acts and allowing time to pass without strangle-holding it with your intense longing, are the only criteria. There are scores of people who have healed their bodies, relationships, financial situation, and completely turned their life around. J.K. Rowling, author of the *Harry Potter* series, was at one point in such financial straits that she and her young daughter were living in public housing and on food stamps. Rowling believed that her *Harry Potter* book series would be a success — she believed it from the depths of her soul — and she was right, and eventually became history's first billionaire author. Others have healed their bodies after injury or illness; still others have their own unique, night-to-day stories. Anything and everything are possible, so long as you imagine, believe and release — and then receive!

How will my manifestation come about?

It is not your responsibility to figure that out. You must never meddle in the middle, but rather allow your desire to materialize according to the universe's operations. Your manifestation may or may not become real the way you thought it would, but what is certain is that the simplest and most straightforward path is the path from your subconscious to your field of view.

I'm on a time crunch. Something happened this morning and I need to manifest the solution today. If it doesn't happen today, then it won't help me. Can I manifest something in a hurry?

Yes, absolutely! We are not left to our own devices in a cold, computerized universe. There is a Divine presence all around us who knows our situation. Your manifestations *always* arrive at the right time and place. If your situation necessitates a quick solution, then imagine it, believe it is real, and let it go, and you will be amazed at how your issue becomes resolved. Relax and place your trust in the most capable hands and know that your subconscious will project that serenity onto your field of view.

❖

I don't care for my current situation in life, but I am showing gratitude every day for all my present moments. Will gratitude expand and increase my current situation?

No. Life isn't a computerized input-output machine. Your life and your circumstances are known to the Divine. When you show gratitude for your present situation, in spite of wishing it would change, it will change. Gratitude doesn't just expand situations regardless of what they are. Gratitude opens doors, increases and expands pleasures and beauty, and creates new opportunities to grow and become joyful. Gratitude is the best tool in your arsenal for combatting your current rut in life. Showing gratitude for all aspects of your life, presently, will improve it in every way.

I've been going through a really tough time lately, but I didn't consciously imagine any of what is happening to me. None of these events occurred in my imagination, so why am I seeing them in my field of view?

This relates to the power of our beliefs and assumptions, and why it is so imperative to stem the more negative ones from our subconscious. Even though you may never have imagined the specific hardship you are now enduring — and I don't doubt that statement at all — it is your underlying beliefs and assumptions about yourself, and the world which have brought about your current field of view. When we believe, in the deepest crevices of our soul, that life is hardship and we are magnets to tribulation, that is exactly what we will experience. When we harbor fear deeply embedded in our subconscious, even if we are not always consciously aware of it, we will manifest situations which reflect that fear back onto us. Whereas imagination is able to manifest both specific incidents and general situations, assumptions and beliefs lean more toward creating general circumstances — the chapters of our lives.

Developing a sincere and consistent practice of gratitude is the direct antidote to false beliefs and assumptions about the world, and gratitude is the key that will unlock the door and liberate you from your dire straits.

You have done nothing wrong, and you don't "deserve" your hardships. However, you have certainly aided in their development because of your deeply embedded belief system. This life can be complicated, and none of us were born with the user manual. However, you have now been made aware of an awesome power, which in turn comes with awesome responsibility. You turn the ship of your life around immediately by making a conscious, dedicated practice of deliberate manifestation in your lifestyle.

Can I tell people about my manifestation?

It is better to keep your manifestations to yourself, until after they become reality. The more you begin to tell others of your intentions to manifest this or that, people will inevitably tell you to "get realistic" or "that's impossible." These words will weigh you down. Moreover, we live in a fallen world, and some people become envious and jealous even at the thought of another person attaining good. As a general rule, keep your manifestations to yourself until after they become real in your field of view.

After that, you can absolutely tell others about this amazing power, but always with good intentions. Never tell others about your manifestations with the intention of showing off. Tell them your stories so they can be motivated to discover their own power.

Is it wrong to want material abundance?

No, there is nothing wrong with wanting, seeking and achieving material wealth and prosperity. I think people often assume that they are not worthy of abundance, and therefore wanting it is a sign that they are materialistic, hedonistic or miserly. Everything in excess is inadvisable, and because many people have low spiritual self-esteem, they think the bare basics of a nice home, car and wealth are excessive.

You deserve every form of prosperity, and material prosperity is part of your natural birth right. Imagine it and claim it because you deserve it. And, when you receive it, remember to share it with your loved ones.

After I've properly impressed my imaginal acts upon my subconscious, and before it appears in my field of view, what do I do?

Allow it to come. You allow your manifestations to be projected onto your field of view by properly manifesting it, and then waiting for it with full and unadulterated expectancy. If you feel inspired to take a certain action, then go for it, but don't force anything. Embrace the feeling of it already being here, and it will soon be so. That's all you need to do in the interim: feel it here, believe it here, and patiently expect it to show up.

Do my manifestations appear all at once, or in stages?

It can happen either way, but a very good point has been raised. Oftentimes we manifest something, and it comes incrementally. An easy example is money. Sure, we'd all like to win the lottery, but perhaps your subconscious will project wealth upon your field of view in stages. If this is the case, you will soon begin receiving free cups of coffee; you will happen to park by the meter that already had an hour of time left over from the previous car. You will find $5 on the ground and no one around to claim it but you. You will earn a raise in salary — not enough to buy a yacht but enough to satisfy you until the next boost in finances.

This is a very important point to remember. We often think that our manifestations failed because we never experienced a sudden, large happening in our life, but in reality, we were receiving our desires in stages. The more you show gratitude, even for finding a dime on the sidewalk, the more quickly and grander will be your manifestation.

Whenever you find something as small as a dime on the sidewalk, understand that you are on your way, and show gratitude for that. Even if you aren't grateful for the ten cents, which doesn't buy anything these days, be grateful for the fact that you are attracting wealth into your life, even if in stages.

This experience isn't limited to money. Anything you manifest may or may not come in increments. It all depends on the natural order of the world, and upon how your subconscious chooses to project itself upon your field of view.

❖

Made in the USA
Las Vegas, NV
11 October 2022

56994998R00100